Heart Print

JOHN TRANTER

PUBLISHED BY SALT PUBLISHING
PO Box 202, Applecross, Western Australia 6153
PO Box 937, Great Wilbraham, Cambridge PDO CB1 5JX United Kingdom

First published 2001

Printed and bound in the United Kingdom by Lightning Source

Typeset in Swift 9.5 / 13

British Library Cataloguing-in-Publication Data
A catalogue record for this book is available from the British Library
ISBN 1 876857 32 3 paperback

SP

1 3 5 7 9 8 6 4 2

Heart Print

JOHN TRANTER is a leading Australian poet. He has been employed mainly in publishing, teaching and radio production, and has travelled widely, making reading tours to more than forty venues in the USA, England and Europe. He has lived in London and Singapore, and now lives in Sydney.

He has published fourteen books of verse, and has been Visiting Fellow at the Australian National University, writer-in-residence at Rollins College in Winter Park, Florida, and poet-in-residence at Cambridge University. A selection of his poems appears in the *Norton Anthology of Modern Poetry*. He compiled and edited (with Philip Mead) the *Bloodaxe Book of Modern Australian Poetry*, and he is the publisher and editor of the widely-read Internet literary magazine *Jacket*, at http://www.jacket.zip.com.au/

Also by John Tranter:

Poetry

Parallax
Red Movie
The Blast Area
The Alphabet Murders
Crying in Early Infancy: 100 Sonnets
Dazed in the Ladies Lounge
Selected Poems (1982)
Under Berlin
The Floor of Heaven
At The Florida
Gasoline Kisses
Late Night Radio
Ultra

Fiction

Different Hands

Anthologies and compilations

The New Australian Poetry
The Tin Wash Dish
The Bloodaxe Book of Modern Australian Poetry (co-editor)
Martin Johnston – Selected Poems and Prose

To John Lucas

Contents

Acknowledgments

Acknowledgment is due to the editors of the following publications where some of these poems first appeared: 'The Beach', the *Australian's Review of Books*, 'Coffee' *Non* (San Francisco) and *Overland* (Melbourne, Australia), 'Country Matters', 'Lookup Table' *Gare du Nord* (Paris), 'Gallery' *Overland* (Melbourne, Australia), 'Globe', 'My Story', 'Sfumato' *TinFish* (Honolulu), 'Halogen', 'Off Radar' *Shearsman* (Britain) 'Limbo', 'Per Ardua ad Astra' *Salt* (Perth, Australia), 'Locket', 'Package Tour' *Angel Exhaust* (Britain), 'Men's Talk' *New American Writing* (California), 'Miss Proust' *London Review of Books*, 'Pyramid' *Stand* (Britain), 'Serial Numbers' *Cordite* (Sydney), *Sulfur* (Michigan), 'Songlines' *Meanjin* (Melbourne, Australia), *Sulfur* (Michigan), 'South Farm' *Heat* (Sydney), 'Under The Trees', 'Vista' *Boxkite* (Sydney), 'Whitecaps' *Kunapipi* (Aarhus, Denmark). Acknowledgment is due to the editors of the following (mostly Australian) publications where some of the sonnets between pages 81 and 94 first appeared: *the Australian, Blacksmith, Contempa, The Ear in a Wheatfield, Makar, Meanjin, Nation Review, New Poetry, Overland, Poetry Australia, Poet's Choice* 1975 and 1977, *Southerly, Southern Review, Stand* (Britain).

The author wishes to thank the Australian Artists Fellowship Advisory Panel of the Australia Council and the Literature Board (now the Literature Fund) of the Australia Council for various fellowships and grants – the first twenty-seven years ago – without which many of these pieces would never have been written.

Lavender Ink

Look, there she is: Miss Bliss, dozing
in the shade of a Campari umbrella. Beside her
a book – something brilliant: Callimachus,
let's say, printed in an elegant Venetian type –
half-read, with the most alarming
            metaphors to come,

and a glass of gin, a cool dew
blooming on the crystal, the air
            kissing her skin
and the neighbour's hi-fi playing
'I Can't Get Started' in a distant
            corner of the afternoon.

The yachts on the water.
            The tinkle of ice.

I'm thinking of you, reinventing Sydney
a thousand years from now, and not
getting it quite right: missing the
delicate hangover, the distant murmur
of the city, the scent of this ink
            drying on the page.

Black Leather

They had returned to get the acoustic atmosphere
for the movie about the French criminals, recording
the soul of the place. When the narrative dissolved she felt
abandoned: first, as though her friends had walked out on her,
then in the other sense, loose, morally bankrupt.

It was an 'optimistic' picture, but dark.
The main writer fought with the story doctor,
refusing to answer his pained questions. They were
intellectuals, she shouted, don't you understand?
Working all night she developed strategies,

and gathered a close group of friends around her
to fend off the advances of the others, those
godless and tireless plotters. And the pages
whirling in the metallic light above the sand, the
waves and the pages folding and turning.

I could see her problem: the cranial arteries bulging,
bad culture gushing across the blood-brain barrier,
from the pages of soiled old books and splashy
magazines, a dozen new theories every month
boiling to the top of the heap of reprints.

Her students thought they had found a new leader,
the art pumping, and an innocent job, raking in money
and promotion. But the infection was linguistic,
and the form malevolent. She panted in the staff room
like a fly trapped in a Contents Page, struggling

with some half-dozen new hypotheses,
thinking she was checking them out, but
they were doing the checking, sorting out
the designer theories, the gangs of black-clad youths
hunting down the latest clever chat.

Her work was growing stunted and corrupt
but fluent for all that, and people bought it.
The skyrocket of fashion, it's not evil, she said,
it can be useful, even for the working class,
look, they bask in the light from its burning tail.

That's how culture floats on the lake
of civilisation, its image wavering in the hazy air.
She thought of her certain extinction – no –
you'll always win if you can predict how
the dog will jump, her script doctor said.

Memo: When I began decoding the images
unravelling from the screen I thought I was
reading your heart print, but I'd been fooled.
Woman does not have a Soul for a reason,
you argued, it's not the product of evolution,

that fashion for splitting up the dead, they so many,
into burnt or heavenly pensioners, that is vicious,
can't you see that? The projector flickering,
the pages signed with her name curling
in the heat, blackening and bursting into flame.

Coffee

The edge of the fields were green, you could see them
through the narrow streets like a distant movie,
a few tiny people moving about slowly, sowing
or reaping. And in the other direction, a glimpse
between two high white walls, the glass-green sea.

We brought bad weather with us – bluish clouds
blowing across the sky, and a chill darkness
covered the fields, flecks of silver mantling the waves,
storm wrack on the shore. I had a vision
of people descending on this isolated place

at the bottom of the planet, bringing bad manners
with them, manners adapted to a different culture,
survival in the bear-pit of the city, let's say.
We found what was forbidden, isn't that
what we're always looking for, then tossing aside?

So we sat on the oars of the self, and time drifted by.
Along the shore, life balanced exactly on the knife-edge
between the drab and the sublime, 'between the shit
and the champagne,' she said, spying on the town,
cigarette slanting from her lips, binoculars held steady,

the lenses at the front racking and peeping in and out.
'When I was young I led myself into mischief,'
she said. 'High on joy, that's what I want,
and I want anyone's arms around me.' She was
holding a tiny drawing and showing the customers,

then she pulled back. It's building it up from these
tiny pieces, day after day, so that months
turn into years, and it gets done, but so slowly.
She was painting all night, drinking too much –
she put something in it – her boy friend killed himself.

I had gone to the city, the Big Smoke, and
in that crowded beehive my thin talent for being led
led me by the nose to the magazines with the bright leader,
but it's just a job, yet I couldn't tell her that, as if
it were all just cheap drink, at the magazine's expense.

You forget so much. Later there was a tough time,
locked away, I guess, endless winter, you wonder
what he was thinking about year after year –
the rope around the rolled carpet, maybe, the lumpy
body in there – he sank back into his seat

at the end of the show, then the lights were fading.
What I did, she said, I figured I couldn't be nabbed for.
It was above the ordinary, beyond the pale.
She threw down the brush, and started crying.
From the beach hotel to the place of worship, a few

sad steps. 'A glass of water – God help me.'
She could see it all, like a half-forgotten dream.
Coffee was brought to her on the beach.
something like scotch poured into the mug,
that makes you sweat, that makes you dizzy.

Country Matters

I gambled with my body, and I lost, Julia said.
She seemed an angel of the stairs
poking about up there. Did I believe her?
I fell into a deep grabby sham.
The shape of a cross, a faint trowelled reality,

full of sound, and drugs to cure a migraine.
Tony slid down the blurry slope of his anxiety
and disappeared into his misery, floundering.
That was okay by me. I didn't want him
hanging around the new project, spoiling things.

I'd buy and sell a fat parcel of real estate
in the time most folks would take to eat a dinner.
On the stone path that wanders through the copse
a drop of red, then a rusty smear, the colour of nails
buried underground in a dark hole, reddish-brown,

which is the colour of dried blood. I saw a dim thing
struggling into life, unwilling, moving in the currents
under the rocks. I gulped the thick air, then heard
an angel singing, and a lot of medicine bottles
cascading. 'The lamp was dying for lack of oil.'

If you didn't mention writing there was work
to talk about, from some backwoods cache
they've invented folk tales that go on for hours.
First you gather in the back room, then you drink
the rum. So the folk tale begins.

The young couple met at the first milepost
outside town, or so the story says.
The man carefully stole up to the gang, heard
what they were talking about, every little whisper,
then a twig cracked, and they swung around, cursing,

then the clack of a rifle bolt in the silence
of the misty fields, eucalypts dripping, how
the distant shot echoed back and forth
along the sides of the valley, then died away –
Does that make sense? The brief lamp

was my fault, guttering, going out.
Then they all lay back on the seat
and talked about the girls at the local dance,
not hiding their feelings so that anyone
who wanted to gave a history of his passion,

threw himself together in the manner of a manikin
making a soul for himself using psychic pressures
to mould the memories and anger's laser
to model it, the soul being formed at adolescence,
rather than at birth, and why not?

That's when the blazing light of the world
strikes you, and suddenly you're to blame for things.
That it was done and written out for God's sake
is inscribed at the front of the book
thus, in the hope of sanction and forgiveness.

Gallery

The teachers would hammer us into artists,
recalcitrant base metal beaten into gold,
if they could. To me, joy-rides were art,
and ploughing was a type of inscription –
I hear behind the droning motor someone's

childhood weathered away and wasted, the boy
in the threadbare snotty jacket hating us
for noticing him thus, and his blame becomes
his chief addiction, a flush of resentment,
about how others pushed and bullied.

Who's pushing? The theory that pretends to be
no theory at all, it was busy blocking that other
theory, disordered, quarrelling, quickly finished with,
his royal madness noted spotting plots behind the bushes,
sobbing with rage, a devotee of the sulky air.

I lived in grace, and fell into poisoned maturity –
seaside cabins packed with wicked kids drinking –
a world of bush farms turned into a landscape.
To read it, you just moved forward into it.
They call those mountains a 'horizon', which is only

a boundary, not a thing. Parents were templates,
but I could not plot the father. A spanner
clinked on steel and danced in the ringing shed.
The tractor did its work like any rusty mechanism
and his office was the open air, a church of absence.

He wore old blue things. Does history
have to be past tense? The diary says I'm
older than he ever got to be, can it be true?
In a fragment of dream chatter I
catch my voice from another room and hear

my father's laugh. Is he here? He's been dead –
'I had the shivers – lock the back door.' Broken
now – pack away Hope, his poem of the future.
I photographed myself, I drank the rain
in deep gulps in flooded February.

Driving to a party, young people, that cheap kiss
traded for a magazine with torn covers.
High on killing ethylene, I realised
wrong could be right. They'd punish the boys
to save them. I would not join.

You had to take a girl to the dance, or
you were a creep, the guys opined anxiously.
And her? She wanted to be a debutante,
though she knew the routine was a farce.
Kids growing at their own pace, by the river.

The old men forbade the barbecue, and now
a thunderstorm begins with pattering drops,
laughter, girls' dresses bunched under the shelter,
the grey sky stretching so far, impossibly distant,
where I glimpse myself longing to go home.

Globe

In the first chapter a raw wind blew up
and discovered streams of watery alarm,
the reader frozen in front of a silent knife
to escape the due pain, I'm arguing
stimulus-response, or motor inhibition

in the face of the inhuman demands of this print,
that reaches out of some corner of the past –
a grubby back room stinking of tallow –
and orders you to stop thinking like that, now
start thinking like this, and do the things

that are inevitable, given this new
political alignment of wish and fear –
no, let me think about a road that wandered
down the flank of a hill, through thick grass
under the moonlight, snowfields gleaming

on a distant glacier – no, I must read
these halting words that once leaked and stumbled
from the nib – I see them begin their journey
through the post, the type shop, printery,
warehouse, then trucks grunting through

the city streets and then the silence of a bookshelf –
high, almost out of reach, at the back
of the self-help section in the shadows,
towards a happy auditor, or, lensed
and winking glints of light onto the kitchen table

the miserable viewer, I mean reader, hypercritical
at breakfast, and so taunt his target of scribble,
these doodles intersecting with his fate –
what did the Professor say? – a hostile
curl to his lips, nausea – no ballot, no blame.

I felt like an electrical lead, carrying the news
down the cable to the TV hookup.
I could have chuckled at the way he slept
as he grunted and changed position – dreams
decorate the endless competition between

our hopes and what we get, or put another way,
between the good boys we hope we are
and the black thing shrieking in the cellar,
all rage and spittle. It's a ferry – that's it –
to carry things over, from one shore to another.

Theories never know the peaks, they just
endure the drudgery of the climb, then
some other bastard gets all the kudos.
The dealer was really the Professor, in disguise,
forged papers, taking a chance on the thin voice

that spoke economics: he looked up from a globe
where he was plotting his travels, for journalism
or a work of literature maybe, the strange future
that he was about to step into and vanish in –
like having to be a writer for the first time.

Halogen

A cold wind came into the room, it frightened
everyone. It was not only that the temperature
dropped, that chill air blew against my skin, but
now the outside was invading the cute domestic space,
something horrible was blundering in,

a taste of death, a slavering alien, those were the
fucking metaphors that Brain-Damage here
was babbling before she fell onto her martini glass
and cut her abdomen on the broken shards,
the lemon stinging in the wound.

Yes, this is the new lingo, brazen, disfigured,
named after those serrations on the kitchen knives
whose cutting edge is etched by a blade of light, that
apparatus glittering on the altar of the bourgeoisie,
dazzled with adjectives and halogen lights.

You didn't make up with him – there, are you
going to say the whole disaster was my fault, you,
tête-à-fucking-tête with the guard dog on the patio?
Straighten up! I'm not interested in the cave
where your teddy bears are projected on a wall,

the velvet manacles and the various bottles.
Now the open road – grainy black and white –
collapsed, separated by photos, the family sobbed,
shark eat shit and they should never have to read about it
and they had to read about it because your bad deeds

follow you home, the ashamed pattern
slipping down the stairs and colliding with reality.
I'd been within voice range of that wreckage,
cramped by journalism, the politics of friends
reviewing each other in the weekend papers.

It's simply a kindness, isn't it, but looked at
from over the fence, a slick fall from honour.
Friends laughed it off, others were aghast, the critics
said it was greed, and how come I couldn't tell
the difference? Then in the garden, two people

behind the screen, the peaks reflecting late sunlight,
poison into the very mouth, then the necessary nausea
as mustard is pumped in to bring other stuff out,
is there an economy in that?
or a loss of faith? They

were gaping at the wounds in my stomach.
For weaklings, it was too much.
They had slept under the desert moon,
the kiss of the mirror, but under that problem
were others, made visible when the lamps arrived,

head over heels in love, then a sharp pain, and I
made excuses to the medium's creep forward in time.
Then she'd be interested in that reality solicit,
the movies cranking out their smoky humour.
Then everything dissolves, down the river.

Limbo

The boss striding ahead into the meeting
like a top dog into the council pound,
through the darkened glass you could see
the horizon lit with flashes, the smoking city,
thunder rumbling behind the horizon,

no lights on in the room so turn them on,
you might think something was behind the door.
He drove his rigmarole through the troops,
and his voice grew sugary, cajoling,
and the others heard it with a shudder.

Competition was wired into the species.
From out of a limbo of sleep and anxiety
the meeting got started, a coffee, no,
a stiff drink, could you take this down,
Miss Venezuela, or are you too busy?

He felt out of place saying it: we live or die
according to the graph, do you understand?
There's knowledge in the sherry-coloured eyes
of a cow, but what is it? Food? The stock market?
Those dips and sudden swoops, it makes you ill.

In the petrol-coloured eyes of a dog, only
fatalism. Memories were invading, then
colonising his mind. I can go on living here,
she said, miles from town, all alone, that's okay.
Live long enough and you forget David's death,

and the beatings, the police paid to do them.
And then his sister, framed on the mantelpiece,
a dozen years under the ground, forgetting
everything. They kept the telephone connected
in case of emergencies, they hated the voices,

the bell made a sound like a fire alarm.
In the endless silent afternoon she imagined
noises from the shed – was the lock on the snib?
There must be something bad behind the door.
He tried to concentrate. Where was he?

She asked me to write more often, but
I disappeared, like I was a bad dream, and
she never said she was lonely, then she died.
Green Devils printed on the dinner plates,
things our family used to remember, and now

no one will remember them. After dinner,
sniping at the town people, recounting
how they do their various self-destructions.
He shook himself. The aggression of foreign companies,
it seems inevitable, the survival of the most

bastardly is built into the system, he explained,
a dance tune designed to be danced to,
and they don't write songs with an odd
number of feet, they must have an even tempo,
the rhythm of business, do you understand?

Locket

Her laugh had shocked her university friends.
She would have to find a faith in a bottle,
the dark never really dark, but her life story
more like a riddle at the bottom of the glass
calling the loonies in across the lawns.

Crazy smile – I'm a bit of surgery,
this is not my real career, he said; I'm a jockey –
tracing the tram track it followed – my life,
not myself. And worse, his brain was a dick,
that's how he described it. Cut to the economy

of the street, they were just bad, those
cruising boys, the bay now a body locker,
on the nearby slopes a homestead or two,
no traffic on the grass, only on bitumen because
appropriate – driving around in her dad's car and her

usual daze like a robot on Sunday, the slow traffic
photographing how it is reflected as a carnival
by the strips of dusty glass, how the murmur
has a querulous inflection, the tone the T'ang poets
struggled to get down on paper, once they'd invented it –

ages ago. She had taken her name from a ribbon,
a name tag that offered a motto – *loser.*
Then when she broke open the fortune cookie,
the message gave the proof of Fermat's last theorem,
wasted here among the groggy customers.

They were busy calling blue jokes out
to one another in the toilets, yelling through
green glass, and tawny lemon, and the scent
of that cheap hospital grade disinfectant
and she answered: *I'm listening to that,*

you jerks! From a neighbouring cubicle
then – a smaller moment than many –
I knew that she'd sob, that her good times
had ended, that she seemed the strangest creature
to herself. It was so lonely there, in the suburbs

fringing the university, the passing crowd
full of brainy Australian intellectuals who,
once they'd been indoctrinated thoroughly,
had all turned into their own doubles – like that.
She stumbled on her high heels, maybe she would have

developed into a genius, who knows, and her friends
were shocked when the Chinese waiter brought her home,
back early from the old testament, and babbling scribble,
stretched out from each week's work, remember disentangle
her mad laugh at the dark, then looking through the car

for her makeup. Her laugh echoed under the trees,
the lamplit street sleeping, now a dog spoke,
the moon sinking behind the distant ridge,
her university friends abandoned long ago,
along with her childhood – marriage – the locked locket.

Lookup Table

His brain has come unfastened over it,
the problem he wants to be remembered by –
that delicate space between what he'd done
and what he'd meant to do, and how
everyone looked at it differently. He hoped

his children would grow to adulthood
unmarked by childhood guilt, but
what does any of that matter now?
They told her the temples were destroyed,
that the country was ruined by tourists.

She asked if they just heard our engines
turning over and sounding sugary, like rock salt
growing at the end of the alley – 'Hernando's Hideaway'.
The sounds faded away down below. That day
the signal was heard for the first time.

He made it a hard-edge problem and argued with it
until it sparkled – he'd taken a knock on the floor
at a dance marathon – talk to me each week
on the telephone, long distance, remember, red
was a code for everlasting love,

the hue and saturation cycling through a list
of all possible data types in one domain
and she'd say that she had no time for such nonsense,
multiple pattern shifts under yellow leaves, brown
mulch pond ice crack frost cover glow

which is a mirror for that hard blue canopy
small trajectories under glitter
far up where ice whisper is a chalk trace
more pollution, less care, as if the papers mattered
or the cracks gaped and then were papered over

what emerges is bracket or death whisker
now inching forward to the ledge underfoot
what drop what bottle, too soon to know it perfectly
too late to endure history with honour or advantage
this must be put to the side so baby doesn't break it

that must be placed exactly at the intersection
of the noun and the verb, who never touch
but trade through articles and deft ranking
thus, one lower, one degenerate
hollow victory fills up quick enough

on the bank, slippery mud, at the bottom, bodies,
now the sky becomes a plate, now the plate
holds up the century, now the fad is a crack
in the ceramic adjective surface noun
in synch, the locket the socket how the nut rattles

in the metal bucket for just so long as it must cease
to dither adaptive color tables and fall to entropy
thus much no further fuss and blather
first on the highway last to supper
socket from coupling, mike to speaker, speak.

Men's Talk

I was one step ahead of the plausible talkers
but only because I could hardly speak, is that true?
Rolling over the animal streets, singing and yelling.
For example, I had to take one bad person
to hospital, gasoline burns. I've spent a lot of time

at the water lips – drinking at full platter. On the job?
He had some cheek, to reach the wreck so quickly.
The leader ordered the windows broken, never
bring bad feelings into it, eh, Professor?
Batting her eyelashes at me, this dame, uh,

she got the news and came up from Melbourne for nothing
remarkable, but that happened, and soon a rural house. I
couldn't disagree that it adds the flavour of a giggle to
this most serious commitment, passion of a scent job, Beth,
I guess – no, switching – spinning – lost again –

bleeding blue underneath what country? Whose
loyalty said empty speech? A man like that makes friends
easily. And this effort persuades the drab to glitter,
dragging something broken and ugly to a limping elegance
just so some fairies can chuckle over it, who do you

think you are? At the edge of the worn blue collar
the nape of his neck was red where the sun had burned it.
He leaned on the bar, it was cool in there –
I guess these fragments make up the town's speech –
they have their own miniature history, coloured

and tinted by the larger history the big boys own –
those bullies – Boy, that cold beer tasted good,
but only if you work to deserve it, the boss said –
he breaks out the snapshots and laughs, I can freeze
a smile and identify a communist at a tea party –

she became a shark tearing the plot to bits
and she talked Karl Marx at them,
those shopkeepers, and insulted their families –
you didn't make a friend of the working class, it's like
bringing Frankenstein's monster home sweating –

I felt certain he was afraid under that
cheerful smile, and I was right, he killed himself, that
afternoon, was I to blame? That went down as gossip,
what a fine pair of silences, doors sealed with an image
of his face, we'd be interested in the story, sure,

for a price – we're sensitive to that elegant style,
that leaking theory where the palette knife
knows these things and wishes to make a mark,
I had made myself known to the other officers –
the kind of life I had, this was not a nightmare,

but a way of adding value to your life, I had to know
what damage – in the wind that
I couldn't – seemed immune –
knocked the boy down
punishment

Miss Proust

To her the kissing group of husbands and wives
was like a gang of schoolgirls in the laundry,
all fuss and bother, with no proper theory of how
sexuality is conditioned by the economic
strictures of society, and not by the games shows

and the sporting programs or by the lies
that stain the pages of cheap paper, for example,
when her friends told her she was a rotten writer –
fuck it! – plumping up the pillow of her emotions –
so she could feel in love – click on, click off –

and revel in a moody air in the kitchen, scribbling
diary entries as though they were great roiling thoughts
or worse, riveting literature, meant to be read out
during the long night of the adult education course
training tapping dogs to do the new job, it's obviously

made for love, this mechanical device with its ribbon
spooling out reams of confectionery and duplicity
that young women desperately want to believe
could happen to them, like doctors who are stern and rich –
no, *will* happen to them – and the pretty nurses

who are young and whimpering, but somehow dazzling,
the same story, only glowing with a more literary quality –
now it happens, only the ending is wrong,
and the hero, called Bruce or Duane, is a loser –
there are no doctors here, they live elsewhere

with their wives, their investments, and their matched
pairs of children. We went over the story –
in the magazine with the doll on the cover –
her writing was okay, it pulled in the money, but
the 3-D Speed Queen routine she put on

mainly for the benefit of the mirror, that was relatively
thrilling, and her hair, so expensive, like snakes – dark
and full of movement. I've spent a lot
on these magazines, the shameful ones, and
often longed to be a maker of such spectacles,

my hand writing out a kind of existentialism
of the glands – clashing or cooperating – keen
to be liked, anxious to find a friend,
weary of the endless social gambits, sad to admit
the need for wariness and protective latex devices.

I was like a wave in a tiny dry-point etching,
apparently calm on the surface, distressed underneath.
I know it is no excuse, but that angry remark
that was changed into something cool and polished,
like an aphorism, isn't that a betrayal of the emotion

that produced it? Isn't it cultural greed reified,
and turned into a regular income? Answer me,
you little shit! There you are, sobbing,
hiding under a pile of theories in the corner,
dabbing at your makeup and hoping not to be noticed.

My Story

Back in *la belle époque* the hired hand would spend
all his savings on a wireless, and turn a cold shoulder
to the investment bloopers of the rural poor.
You learn enough to get along, the rest
is embroidery bracketing mushy urban wishes.

Stared at by the sun some freckled tomboy
wants to buy a drink, but she drops her change –
a coin rolls into the gutter and down the drain,
unimagined voyages to distant Floridas strapped
to the wheel of the will, where the water boils

in the teeth of the hurricane – never to happen,
dark and cold while the centuries roll overhead.
Now some rustic is rubbing my face
with his nicotine-stained fingers. Token?
They won't remember what the cycle meant.

Winter nights... the village draws the snow rug
around its knees, the lamps whisper nostalgic
baloney from one side of the street to the other,
the old schoolteacher peers at his book –
the book which talks of glory, and later

he'll be reduced to getting drunk on beer and
watching football through a tube –
Think of an accordion bought and sold – boy,
it must have seen some parties! Or imagine good times,
bad times, around the pianola. A rat doesn't need

a degree in entomology, he just carries the plague,
it's his talent and his gift. This is just one coin,
but it speaks for its millions of brothers, gazing
down on the planet through the polished
lens of commerce: tides, movements,

the harbour mouth silting up. It must be
phenomenal to be a farmer, every nerve in your body
in touch with the seasonal interest rate fluctuations,
doing your bit to clog the rivers and pollute the earth,
and, given a flexible borrowing rate, able

to rent a light plane to spread insecticides
almost on a whim – ploughman as artist. Now
the bond ratio climbs, now a family
plunges into debt and alcohol,
now the Red Man is pressed from this

part of the West, miles of waving sorghum
cover what was once a prairie, now in Kalamazoo
a bookkeeper plots to bring down a bank.
The earth revolves, hiding its secrets. I may sleep
for a million years, and when I turn up at last

my value will be infinite, or nothing. What drugs
will replace me? My story, a sixpence
shaped like the moon, always standing in
for someone else, the soft suffering flesh
put behind me, part of a stupendous machine.

Off Radar

I tried selling – a dog would sell better.
Then I dived into escape, relaxation –
westerns, flirting at the local dance, cheap
fiction, I said I was an expression of the times,
nothing more – bring a jug of water –

and the hicks spinning on the sawdust floor
believed me, drinking in the music, the glitter and
the harsh saxophone ambience which belongs
to our century, the minor chords Bach didn't know –
because artists feel more deeply they have a special

right to authentic orgasm – enough teaching,
I know the law as nails understand
the hammer – my focus set at the horizon,
racking in the light, inch by inch by inch
then the sun came up, the sky a deep blue –

what happened out there, it was not so much
a hairstyle as a wig, and this kind of thing
happened to Australian art every year,
talent moulting, sheep sheltered from the sun,
fading like the shadow of a phobia, less nexus,

more periphery – one daydream concerned
the pitch-black truck manoeuvre, the acid bath.
Again and again how sheer the brand-names
and cliché kisses, boycott knocked rocking –
you can't wrench free of the devised world –

there's my wife, sad old neighbourhood angel,
she never got jealous, never ran down the other,
the innocent one – God help me – blizzards
that he believed made her happy, an arm
around her, is that sad moment over? – hey

sweetheart, did your husband hear the boy paint?
I drew on pliable acetate, now it's
a subtle cheater, where my ambition
was to have a stimulant stab at his work,
my shirt pocket full of pencils, brain

full of plans for escape from the Lawn Club,
the wives gathering around to graze and feast
on my exoticism, but that was accidental, not
fundamental, back home I was a nobody,
when I need to I can swear to that, and

when it suits me I can be that other person.
I return to the inner sky and the screen flickers,
then clears – they say art tore their spirits to bits –
their howls came after the furiously sobbing girls
woke up to find themselves in their sixties –

mayhap in my childish breast the clock,
an artifice that suffocates – wallpaper, perfume, I'd
cancel the jasmine-scent of radar writing and that's
nothing compared to what we find at the end:
a ring from the little bell on the front of a bike.

On the Road

We met at the bar concealed behind a false front
in the alley behind a curtain dyed purple and green
down the stairs to the shuttered room baking
in the Summer of Love, a country girl, dark glasses,
thirty feet of cedar bar stacked with drinks

but we already had those drinks, and it seems
in the pool of liquid on the bar surface,
after I finished pawing at her soft willing body,
I could see the outline of a face. Too close.
She joined a big city firm, designing perfume,

can you believe, and she used to say 'You have
a soul, in the Big Town, because people let you live.'
Why are these problems linguistic?
That's all we have, to frame the chaos with,
the big grid we drank with our mothers' milk

with the cornflakes and the funerals. This went on
in front of the runaway truck of culture
loaded with 'fashion', that abstract policeman.
It's the beach, dozing on the edge of my mind,
a life hung loose by the water, a giggle of a man

mumbling about the knife-edge of darwinism
hacking at our schools, and what was in the sand,
kids punching each other in the surf –
now from the back of the bar the lost cry
of someone losing out to the sixties, coded

into the static you can hear hissing in the car radio –
God and the Sheriff sharing a good cigar,
entente cordiale, agreeing they love a dash of
green, humanised water with their bourbon.
One chemical strips the other of information,

mingling in the tank of brew. It was lonely,
in the banking business, like a convalescent pushing
a truck uphill, inch by inch, and dog eat dog
in the bull pit, wondering who had the trend brackets
with the right linguistic spin to win.

Then that maelstrom of bad writing
calling students to their doom. 'I didn't
disillusion my poor charges,' the old guy sobbed.
Why do I remember this? He was too much
like me, and I saw my father in the mirror,

growing sad, he had a tale to tell me urgently,
but I couldn't hear, or stay to listen.
I moved out of bohemia, Kerouac went mad there,
that's a lesson, then he died at his mother's,
that's another lesson, to do with philosophy,

Catholic childhoods, bad drink, Oedipus.
I dreamed to cope, and I'd seen what happened,
in the future, like a train becoming larger.
'Here in the present we're just waiting for history
to run us down. Teachers cannot help us.'

Package Tour

There's a gap electricity leaks across
between the eyeball and the page, between
the demonstrator showing off the dicing knife
and the tired woman going home on the train.
For five million people Paris is a place to work,

not a fucking vacation. So the young flirt
went to Europe, meaning to spend her money.
Cigarette packets, rain showers, Existentialism
blowing through the groups of confused tourists –
whistling some tune, these prisoners of air,

a sad little melody that spelled out how
lost they were, under the European weather.
She walked in the rain, the acid drench
that was pouring on the new wet paint,
wading through sheets of green gauze.

Her anxiety was quickly dispatched, and the messages
soon sparked down the wire to clang the bell
back home. The hot air was shuddering, they said
it was necessary – voice flattened by the phone –
to make an example of the rapist feller;

and the girl reporter read about it on the Teletype
and came down here looking for trouble.
We gave her trouble, more than she planned on.
Click. I guess it was some family habit.
She was working class, all right.

You could tell, under the cunning accent
she put on, something hollow, stained, fake.
Everything in the kitchen could be overheard.
To paint – that's all she wanted to do,
even if was just grasping lies.

You could take it that this was only a moral lesson,
or you could imagine more. That's up to you.
She pushed the doors open, looking in
at the confused diners, and only a moment ago
she'd been fascinated by history's obsession with itself,

how we stayed up and talked till dawn
when we were just dumb kids, like philosophers.
She drank ouzo and retsina until even the Greeks
wouldn't have any more of her, drank
till dawn, threw up, then drank some more.

It had been raining in the square,
the cobbles were slick, and coming home
from another binge, she slipped, twisted her
ankle and knocked out a tooth on the kerb.
So the biographer says.

She wore a raincoat everywhere, a matter of
style, to work, to the toilet, God knows, and
when she let it slip to the floor the buckle clacked
on the tiles. She saw her future rise up, a sheet
of lightning. Paris or Peoria, it's all the same.

Per Ardua ad Astra

I was thinking about what happened when you were
a kid, the theft of capital, how the bottle
came uncorked, and how the precious essence
of capitalism simply turned into vapour
and disappeared, destroying whole nations.

It was bookkeeping made it happen,
we should blame the strings of numbers holding
hands, and the passion to build a toy that works.
Capital, it just grows out of the world's matter –
a nugget, a heap of rice, a busload of workers.

I always had my staff learn only the essentials.
More than that, and they develop longings.
Perhaps a Buddhist could offer a better response
to the way the economy is like a ravening animal,
wounding and maiming the poor.

But then, the stragglers have to get picked off,
is that what you said? So let's armour ourselves,
let's get a degree in little things, like courtesy
and social stratagems, how to knot a rhyme,
and dazzle the old ladies with our manners.

The first year I knew her she gave me
the entire history of her mind from go to whoa,
how she faced up to the great cliffs
of European culture, that had destroyed
more than one civilisation, and might do again.

She was confused by truth when it is stacked up into
blocks of history, though not by the lies that
make up politics. I'd been fascinated with mahogany jazz,
you know the stuff, disturbing, dark, but mellow –
but we only heard a mournful song play, and

as the harmonies tangled deliciously and then
unravelled they seemed to say no, to forbid
a country girl to have such thrilling insights.
Or literature, the alphabet pretending to some
great passion, one more bourgeois jerk

raking in the dollars while he tapped at the keys,
constructing a profiterole cloud-castle of emotion –
as vital as a college diploma, this talent for cheating –
though what chance that had of persuading anybody –
no, I'm not jealous – give it a rest – the nerves –

'Neal was enormously attractive to people
who sat on their ass most of the day in a dim room,
biting their nails, and typing out shit.' That's
what he said. He was a big handsome feller,
thick as a brick, whacked on speed most times,

and faintly talented. I couldn't get him hunting, the old
President said – what he was afraid of was a mystery to me,
shaking while the sound travelled low over the ground,
reading The Declaration of Independence through
the telescopic sight on the barrel of a gun.

Pyramid

We heard her voice murmuring, and we must have been
dreaming ourselves awake into movement, a car gliding.
As you mix a drink, you make a friendship, the moon
says, prying into the apartment, excuse me, this
beach shack outfit with communists next door,

and all evening the blather from their radio.
There house meetings were a pond of hostile feelings
about artists, those were the wasters, she working
at a dramatic sideshow by the sink. Then hubby was
back from Korea, and the townsfolk

chiding her about her taint of traitor ideology
tilting to the course of socialism, a moral mudslide.
The photo showed him hunting through
his assembly of idols, the killing machines,
the kissed guy fooling around. So fish thugs out.

A sea of humour, write that on the mirror. She
waved a price stamper, but not every sticker took.
She had the number – temperate, it was politic
gestures advocating war. I've spent too much time
here to waste more on these poor visuals.

Oh the jolt rising over the moonlit horizon
loud porch crowd we drank the decade away
down the ebony wall of the endless party
where the underclass saw humour,
we were that group of losers and a

movement back into the past under the glass.
I'm a chic hint to your career, can you read that?
Climbing, not falling. That price tag their dope,
the bigger the better, and hear the howling desire
now the plane beach, wreckage and she

hurts the best stratagem, my sibling throat.
Let's see how his working could damage me,
I was green and it reflected on this affair, this
hot sound turning smoky, noise darkening
as the creating wind blew by, roaring.

I made up to the town she dreaded, and
the harbour. Their hands were full of those pals,
owing them favours, gifting, and now
they came to colour the town red, but
the townspeople threw up the shutters.

Are they my pals? Old fudgers! Lost again!
He fell on the floor of the pub, like the others.
Under fugue arguments, the drill, the latch.
She put up what the darkroom left her.
So I left, I want to know the studies, the leader

orders and the boom follows, I didn't believe
how your sadness is repeated, this or the other
spectacle. I got you impersonators long on intimacy
and they drew away. He was fading, sinking, failing
the judgment of the water pyramid.

Serial Numbers

And tell the truth – the tumult of various expendable
business plans, and the evening blinked in like a landing jet,
apparently graceful, in fact screaming nuts and bolts –
shaking metal plus desire equals travel industry bond
finance downturn explains his desperation –

he never got over the way his father hated him,
and shook a fist at himself in the mirror, rushing out
to join his pals at a gathering, cheese and wine
and social exchanges a whirling confetti – for a moment
the pack of snarling gibbons recognised something simian

about the crowd at the book party, their embraces
heartfelt yet somehow insincere – talent
given muscle by a bicycle pump, show biz
slang and chatter bouncing off the plexiglass –
model twaddle, chop throttle, sling hash and babble –

there – a thin Singaporean speaking gently
into the handset about the banking
teletype network linking the island republic
to a pit of treasury dread in Yokohama – banknote
suction whirlwind – the old investment managers

fuck up due to lack of basic training in futures hedge
management – chattering over the sherry in between
profit and loss is not the safety rope,
he'd chosen to be an alcoholic, heavily crinkled,
a choice made up of thousands of little weaknesses

day by day, wearing down the rock of his self-esteem.
The young professors traded gossip and influences
– I had lunch with Mister Hartford – oh, really? – just
lunch? – like kids with cigarette cards and pictures of Batman
when they should be practising their knots and lanyards.

Now the secret no one talks about – lack of talent.
You see? Dead quiet. Her suit was a fashion
gesture, while the quay water alfresco wavelets
wobbled through those long railing antlers, bracket,
I mean, slicing up the light into vertical samples,

each related to the one parallel, drawing energy
from each other, a team of singing brothers –
one dollar smells like its sibling in the wallet – print,
print – there's a ferry wandering and churning the surface
now sprinkled with rain. The thunder there

hypnotised – widespread, miniature, far ranging –
flattering the city with dreams of a distant time
when everything was hunky-dory and a hamburger
was something to get excited about. Not the saxophone,
not the forgotten instruments, the cowbells

across the evening pastures, shit on the boots,
or the dew like crystal points on the morning radio
news traffic report not needed here, no traffic,
nothing happens in this town that God don't
know about – he's dreaming it, and we're Him.

Sfumato

Anne you are falling in love late in love,
your life dwindling like an image on the ceiling
traced with a smoking candle, now fading –
at night the stars caught in the tree branches –
they were playing the kissing game, she insisted,

so we felt crazy, the heat, our bodies shackled to shock
smelling the brightest perfume, but she said,
Oh, there, the boys, look, and they murmured
alone together – brown ink on the yellow pages,
lemon playing against the pale blue air,

and she passed around my 'show you' heart,
looking and looking, shopping to buy, the one
who mattered smiling with his eyes, not his heart.
'Once my hopes had died nothing mattered, but then,
when had it mattered?' Too much drinking,

a vista sweeping beyond the plain around
the periphery of the bay, he wiped her mouth,
it was from the summertime fun and drinks,
that and the purple ink on the marriage contract.
So they talked, so he fell arse over heels in love,

he thought she was unattainable, but she ate him up,
is that any kind of a future for a grown man?
He flushed warmly and dragged me past a large
store dummy as he whispered his dirty little secrets,
even the slightest indications of domestic intimacy,

the kind of perfume she used in bed, viruses
and lack of sleep from the trip home,
eleven hours from L.A. across the Pacific.
We made money, we found her an innocent job.
Tie the knot properly – I guess you know to do that –

of course I know – but politics soaks in
everywhere, exposing feelings of desolation.
It was the boss who stole from the customers,
she said, and as far as reporting it to the cops,
she was game. Then security code-words

flashed onto the screen – 'When I believe,
how I believe, what I fucking-well believe – '
is that any way to talk to a superior? It happens
all the time, but knowing about it is different
from doing something about it – my career,

I noticed the old wine had the same flavour
as the stuff the girl was drinking. It made me sick.
Oh yes, you could say it was kind of her.
He told her, over and over, how to teach others
intellectual games, how to sidestep the moral issues,

how to brush up your magnetism and influence people –
held in his stare she was like a fish, somehow.
A snapshot gentility, decayed from the backing sheet
to the front gloss, and now whenever I look at
my career, it's to wonder how I ever believed all that.

Songlines

The rendezvous – did I miss it? I hear a lonesome
whistle – after the gust of miscalculation
steered back on track, leaves publish
quaint borsalino eloquence as today
becomes tomorrow – some paralysis, some

gesture of reproach: 'fuck you!'
the real point of which lies in the gap,
the translation from dim intent to
'that's obvious!' to retrospective explanation –
reverse subjunctive – 'he would have meant...'

then the story of mankind, the babbled
speech in the kitchen – one more whisper,
one less problem to deal with out back,
on the plain of arbitration that stretches
into the haze, distant, endlessly rocking,

tiny adjustments, until the parcel of hesitation
is wrapped up, the way a board meeting
winds down, go home, lights out, lock up,
yet the reason is not explained by the minutes
a troubled secretary attempts to transform into

a final justification for the nature of evil
growing out of an absence of positive good,
that is, it's your fault – who else? for
growing up into something damaged,
not at all what the relatives expected.

What did they insist on at the school assembly?
How the little bracket fits to the left, how
you must be silent at the back of the class.
The song lines – hear them moaning
behind the wind from the sea as it groans

over the beach and up into the dry hills –
the four-dimensional arrays of speech extend from
the bandstand to the knot of quarrelling drunks
in the dark and their chorus of grief blotted out.
The dog didn't bark, to give him a nature,

and thus explained everything, but only
to the smart guy. Now the moon
with slow sad steps ascends its tower
while a pale nothing is spoken above
the silent clearing: a few couples look up,

remembering a misspent childhood, and
an awful noise begins, a clattering
that clambers up over the horizon –
we've left the sobbing secretary behind –
loaded with a kind of message, a porridge

of popular music and bad news announcements
and always the weather at three-minute
intervals – and now I remember what the city
looked like, back then – glorious – meet me
at the station, honey, don't be late.

South Farm

You get yourself a beer from the fridge, pour a glass,
and stand, watching the froth settle, remembering –
or you're leafing through a magazine at the dentist's,
and you see a colour photo of a fox in a forest –
I was after this fox, he said, looked everywhere.

Clever bastards, they know more than you do.
I must have walked four miles through the bush.
I took a rest on this big hollow log. Lovely morning,
dew on the grass, everything quiet. I rolled a smoke,
very peaceful. Heard a noise, looked around,

and the bloody fox shot out of the log
and off into the bracken. I just laughed.
Remember? Dad's laugh had a special resonance,
his voice, relaxed, the rhythm of breath – I hear it
sometimes, now that he's gone, long gone

from the land of the living, smoke up the chimney,
I hear it sometimes at a party, from the next room,
and I go in to look, anxious, excited – no,
there's no one there, except myself in the mirror.
The drink – it's just something to get you started,

breaking the ice of the held-in talk. He said
a rabbit would stretch the meagre rations
during the war – which war? – baked in milk, very
palatable. And the old radio on the kitchen table
was thronged with the noise of the city celebrating,

far away behind the eucalyptus-crowded hills,
and yet close enough to touch. The traffic drone
came from behind the scenery, the urban horizon,
fixed about so high, and there were closer sounds –
talk, murmurs, the noise of people shopping.

Are you just passing by? I whispered – for they
had an odd look: just visiting the planet – aren't we all?
And that struggle, growing up, dying,
what does it matter now? His son
had read the story he particularly liked –

the whish of passing tyres on the street outside
seemed to spell out a message – that he was doomed
to linger in this dim room, lonely, bored,
trying to understand the television that seemed to be
speaking another language to the furniture

until he could be rescued by his family – only
one problem – he didn't have any family.
I am my father's son. In the empty kitchen
the crockery was cold, the dishwasher had stopped
long ago, the detective reasoned – he'd retired

from his position examining the books
for this so-called library, what a laugh, and now
he was raking over the detritus of a life spent
trying to farm stubborn soil. Take me
back to my real parents. I am that detective.

Under the Trees

The boy had been killed, an accident, and how
his parents lived on is hard to understand.
The teacher wiped her misted glasses primly,
and we wheeled our bikes down that long empty road.
My dad, he cranked the handle, holding his thumb

in a special grip he taught me, useless gift,
and the truck started in a cloud of blue smoke.
The candor – that thing I am aiming at –
pungent smoke, memory trace, the jacket –
the no man's land between what I meant to say

and my doleful history – that gap, slot, error –
a body down there in the gully, or floating
in the dam, the boy stumbled on the step
between master and mister, a dreadful threshold.
Stunned, down there among the bracken, resting

just on twilight, then the teacher's broken voice
climbing up through the aether – this ascent
is like a plane, equivalent of hope rising
the way the sunrise gets plants awake –
now just a whistle rising through the static.

The old bell made us wait, life piling up
on the steps outside. How does it matter now?
'My brother,' he said, 'volunteered for service
in the fire brigade, but he was one of them,
the wicked ones, lighting fires and putting them out.'

When they caught him – one story, just one,
from all those countless texts that shape a pearl
layer by paper-thin layer, trochus embroidery,
watered silk of his moods, this is literature?
Under the floor a manuscript rolled up

and tied with string and sealed with wax,
just talk from the city, café babble, passions
nudging at the future like a fish in a bottle
I remember, condemned by the invisible wall,
why didn't I apprehend the future? Tomorrow and

tomorrow staggering into life, and plans
aborted each evening, then an accident to prove
you shouldn't have wanted anything.
You drive past the tree split by lightning
holding up its arms, a piece of burnt wood

in the figure of a ghost watching the forest
as the rain colours the world dark grey and glossy,
something is waiting under the branches, an alien spirit,
the ghastly revenant invaders feel, their own reflection
projected on the ruin they have made.

But looking back, the photograph album, sepia
waterfalls, a wasteland of dead white trees,
the dusty ferns and the cane furniture – outside
in the sun, two magpies quarrelling, saying
'today is all that exists, and be grateful for it.'

Vista

The nurse said something in dialect and looked
down at his body on the bed – gazing fluently.
So dialect structures meaning, but it's hard.
He was poor, asleep, in a cage,
but that was where he wanted to be,

volunteered to be there, chained
to his desk and his duties (teaching)
and (researching) things out of books,
what kind of a life is that, for a man?
The big oaf on the screen chortled and kicked

the fire. Play the guitar, break a few plates –
that's how a man should live! Drink,
make love, sell a little life insurance
while you still have the strength! Zorba
the Geek, laughing in the rain. The accident

happened because of the storm, the moving view
was washed off the windscreen, then replaced –
now the wipers speak their beautiful dialectic,
left and right, dirty and clean, air and water –
he cried at the loveliness of it all! A beat-up car,

teaching him philosophy! He wiped his face.
And religion is like the traffic, he reasoned,
struck by the generosity of this foreign city –
what was I saying? God speaks like a Mack truck,
that voice a diesel exhaust – but does it all

have to work 'like' a simile, every thing
echoed by its ideal form in the underworld?
Am I going there, where the human race
learns its lessons at last, when they can't
do any more harm? The nurse spoke

and adjusted her stiff dress – the sunlight
spoke briefly to the window, of landscapes –
flipped her little upside-down watch
dangling on its pin, and gasped – looked at her
ghost hovering in the glass in front of the view –

the landscape was full of people speaking English
and going about their lives – Carolyn,
that was her name, and she pulled
the toggle to illuminate the lamp shaped like a
planet, then she sent him home with a bottle

of medicine – you wish – they present her
with the farewell gift – no, the superannuation
token – clock, racket – remember how
a flying saucer doused the headlights – the buzzing
sound of everything being switched off –

Carolyn the nurse – dutiful is part of the definition –
stumbling and dropping her champagne
and the metal bowl, the tablets. Well, maybe
she was a doctor, the aliens reasoned, she
spoke their language. What does it matter now?

Whitecaps

To be a stroller, taking in the city from the street,
that clamour and bumping rush with pools of silence
in eddies under escalators and so on, that takes
lots of money, or the dole – a good cigar,
or a rolled cigarette stuck to the lip. Now we see

shopgirls in failed department stores embarking
on their evening dreams as one embarking
on a silver boulevard, sometimes they lie about it,
the dim wishes – if they don't, poverty gets them –
so, a handsome doctor, canoodling on the beach,

moonlight tinted to expose a cheat at supper
on the lawn by the pool, lots of waiters, so we
made love she said, during the afternoon siesta,
outside, thunder, a man sweeping the yard –
a set of gestures called employment – perhaps

a detective hired by my husband, she said, no,
it was just motel security – I could hear
something like a distant marimba playing
through the sonic curtain of the rain.
I grabbed the bottle, held it to my chest,

brilliant thoughts imprisoned in green glass
explicating, in a morning, the follies of philosophy –
I didn't become disillusioned about drink,
it had its job to do. She only seemed immune –
ash littered the table and the carpet – a snapshot

of a room – she explained the gloom, it's
part of how the whole society sinks into the future –
once you had hope, now you see what happens.
And romance novels sucked in a crowd
sobbing and laughing on their way to work,

and now a boat tips over on the windy lake,
whitecaps materialising and disappearing quickly,
bungalows tumbled and floating in the brown flood,
as the upturned dinghy drifted past a countryside
made up of acres of tawny grass combed by the wind,

chilly and quite uninhabited. That lack is awful,
the sky just as empty and uncaring. Now we see
the whole horrible scene printed on the plate glass
of a shop window, now the crowds obscure it,
busy, rushing to their individual fates, now

as we turn away to contemplate the fateful mess,
now that the meaning of it sinks into my stomach
like a crowbar – ash your cigar – I am here,
I am still here – printed on my memories, a watermark –
I remember we paused now and then to keep

our intimacy on the back burner, and most
Friday nights were rough, noisy, cattle in the bar,
gangs of cowboys – she reached into her past,
that silent maelstrom, too late, desperate to find
a future she could live in forever.

The Alphabet Murders

1

After all we have left behind
this complex of thought begins
a new movement into musical form, much as
logic turns into mathematics and automatics
turn into moonlit driveways – 'form at the edge
of hearing', almost, like a locomotive whistle
late at night becomes a linguaphone and then
jumps into bright focus like a lunatic
aware that hunger concentrates the mind
and means lunch straight away – we mean
poems right away and no fooling.
So I write to you 'from a distant country'

2

Before this complex thought begins attacking
what we have left behind – riddles, packaging –
itself must generate enough good luck for the whole voyage.
After trunkfuls of bullshit dumped overboard
and the page alive with noise and verb geometry
I'm ready and lunch jumps into sight and we are off
like a rocket, zooming through the lecture hall where
history becomes a kind of thick paralysis and breaks
down into spasms and morality and all we can remember
through the fog of confusion is how we thrilled
and brought back memories of Captain Marvel
wriggling on a pin, or in the lens' meniscus
held to the niggling eye.
No more literature. The dream is done.
But take precautions: oil the gun, unsheath the pen
and grease the new appointment if you will
for we are not all as easy as the one who hides
in the shadow of the sun and clicks the shutter
at the briefest flick of eyelid or the wettest smile.
I have been keeping a dopey vigil in the tower
to show I'm not mad and making notes
as to the behaviour of the 'lesser sex'. Take care,
I'm winding up the broken clock and being jovial
as though the word 'maunder' held a secret
in its fist – though these dreams are laughable
they grow out of today's economics
and the predestined machinery of the streets.

3

Cool it, with all the friends of scholarship to hand
there should be little fright, so take it easy
riding through the night. Now
the craftsman turns away from domesticity
with its pattern of submission, cliché and reproach
and retires to a house in the countryside.
It is English, autumn, smoky and reposed,
badgers wander across the great lawns in the evening
and the peaceful rhythms of another, better life
claim him piece by piece. He sits musing
in front of an open fire, sketchbook at hand,
as the tapestry weaves its message in the shadow chambers
at the rear of that condominium we call his brain.
Is it inspiration? Is it luck? Is it duty,
that sour globe of perspiration on the nerve?
He grows, the nimble fingers fly, the pattern
reels an arabesque across the paper. Five years later,
with a hearty laugh, he is gone from the country;
then abroad – there are rumours of a sighting
in Dogubayazit, in northern Turkey,
and after that, nothing. And the tapestry?
It is now a joke, a dirty parable
that kids laugh about in school, it is a lesson
that everybody hears and no one understands,
it now hangs in Texas in a renovated castle
and entertains the visitors immensely,
and like some long and boring poem by Matthew Arnold
in which the bloodstained burning battlements of Art
rise up in Hauteur from the sodden Turf
it puffs itself up and explodes all over the onlookers.
It is a bladder bloated with its own conceit, and yet,
rhymed or free, retarded or advanced,
as the poetry of life spirals upward in the smoke
from this great and almost mythical work of art
the skills of horticulture carry on, a million clerks
fill out a questionnaire, the grand pursuit of excellence
convicts itself of nothing, and is praised.
So in his Tartar yurt, his books abandoned,

he becomes the amateur and once again
begins that climb through craft to frightful insight
while all I can do (me! me!) is eat page after
page of this 'plain speaking' in a rhetoric
dazed with ambiguity. You might say that
no career is adequate to my melancholy, as it's
true that no whip is suitable
for my desire, but that's all bullshit
and a different kind of western movie makes it clear.

4

Drifting through the gritty, adolescent Western novel
we find a boundless buried geography jutting up
just underneath the reader's attention-span.
The annual outing of the Literature Society was held
on the foothills near the Epic Volcano, an area
noted for its inhospitable terrain and noxious gas...
Suddenly the mountain-side shudders, belches
and blows up with a lewd cracking noise,
showering the explorers with hard poetry turds.
These little fragments of lyric
fall like tiny brains from the sky
fertilising the lakes and great rivers.
The heavy unpeopled fields that lie
sodden under the mass of tangled verbiage,
the banks of snow that scud back and forth, these
outward symbols of the mind's recalcitrance
plunge us into thinking again and again
and we drive deep into trouble with our queer friends
in the hope of meeting something vast and possible.
What's it like in there? Do we need confidence?
Is a casual knack enough? And we fade away.

5

Ecstasy is the Master of Lunacy and calls the tune
you said, and when he sweated on the bed you retold
some of the ancient craftsman's memories:
'The boats broke against the breakers, and though
we came to the coast in the season of storms
we had wounded warriors, and the sail torn. At dark-fall
rocks dropped down from the cliff, one breaking
the decking, though without great damage.
Behind the border, burning beacons,
thus we were worried where to wend on our going.
We wanted green water beyond the reef.
These are the feared: water, fire, rock and foe.'
All that babble gone down the chute of years
and now a tale to stop up little frolic.
A gaggle of story-tellers followed into folly.
How do we sort it out? The gilded lie,
the tempting truth about a pretty boy
who gambled with a mighty tongue and lost his wits?
('as one hog lives on what another shits...')
'The wild men were hidden half out of water
behind the highest rocks of the reef, and with the longboat
low laden, many made the deck. There was much killing,'
tells the chronicle, though without regret.
What would the Norsemen say? being
busy at their butchery, a kind of trade,
and having neither need nor knowledge of remorse.

6

Fate is a variety of religious experience which is
always asking its own questions, for it is only
a reductive problem, or the essential gesture
behind every question that a little boy might
store away for the future when he stands up
in the midst of the great Lesson and testifies
'I doubt that there's a problem left that hasn't
crawled beneath a book, protecting its value
in the manner of a whimpering aristocrat
in the year of the "Red Tide", or can we only bleat
being so deprived of images by greedy Futurists
(of how the Duke of Money sucked a spanner
and called it infinite delight, surpassing beauty...)
or whether radical gestures
of the more political kind are fit
too neatly to the hawker's palm and politician's arse
and are thus rubbed between the two as if
the only love we were permitted by the Sonnet
was onanistic and deprived, or is it
hope to crawl out of the hole that language
laid us in?' He is not a child, his face
is rainy by now and the class dissolved, he has
forged a destiny from the language and his teachers
must decide to punish him and lead him on
into those areas of doubt and sickness where he grows
suddenly beyond their narrow estimates and breaks
their shackles and the test record and
breaks into a valiant and vacant freedom.

7

Get lost: it might work in a stable society but don't
try it here sonny; we're on the lookout for mistakes
you'll be the first to go we generate
information in the bowels of the earth
and call it 'Happy Holiday, my Good Consumer!' –
the heart abandoned and the tongue forked,
the language binary and don't complain –
we eat 'journalists' for breakfast and 'authors'
for dessert, and if you're clever you're a digit.
You will be pleased to learn we have philosophy:
'No line of syllables can satisfy the Sonnet's
greed for flesh horizons. One dawn repeats
another morning as though metal mocked, becoming
several typewriters at once, and, uh, the
identity code to generate multiple patterns
of rhyme in the cavities of the computer's fear.
Mmmm... music, like a river full of dead
vegetables, and that smell like ice on the vein,
and that paradise of shops. You can make it.'
We came back to that liner
who drew the line at the unreachable horizon.

8

How are we locked into the forme that is
history in the making? At night, when
the mothy lamp flickers and shadows crawl
across the lawn, we dream of a perfect history
and pray that our children will be included
in the small reward that trickles out of action.
Is it too late to stare at ourselves cruelly as we must
if we really want that freedom, or are the little fears
that grow out of human contact and avoidance
and the knowledge of all those terrible old stories
too much even for the willing soul? How do our
acts and gestures, falling through the years,
shore up the silly things we do, the way we
argue and cause pain and hurt our friends with lies,
and make us grand? Grander than we deserve, we think,
and then sob and break down and no guiding hand...
for we have chosen to be free and quite abandoned
and, like a salesman driving to a crucial meeting
in a new convertible, hoping that the number
in his pocket will lead not into labyrinths of choice
but rather to the much-deserved promotion he has
grown accustomed to through books and television
and who imagines dialling and the sweaty phone and
the avalanche that middle age and masturbation brings...
like that small and smelly man we lose hope
just at the city limits and give away the game.
For history is a kind of city, dusty in the quarter
where rats and garbage bury our best illusions
so that something old is seen as something broken
and ignored, and any fresh idea or politician's trick
glints over the rim of the new developments
where orphans, children of ourselves and kin
to those we now imagine, play in a cold
and futile light that sweeps in from the sea
reminding us of those even further reaches
where shapeless things toss on a dark wind.

9

I find myself alone in a room full of stupid poems
I have a searching pain in the neck
I am going to move to Bermuda where
I believe life is innocent and in the pink
I find the pain congratulating itself
I have some of the questions and a bank account
I know how to kill a rabbit and a lobster differently
I know each lives and dies according to its kind
I think constantly on those who were truly stupid
I don't think we've met I'm sorry was that your
I've had enough of 'literature' God damn
I'm caught in the throes of a merciless poem
I'm having a ball I said look out
I don't have any answers isn't that what they say?
I'd certainly love to is that all right?
I am always about to make a serious study of the word
I, and it's always just too late goodbye Mister President
I'm sorry we never met I could have healed your wounds
I think occasionally on those who were truly great
I hope you like the puzzle that
I sent – goodbye Superman goodbye

10

Justice is a kind of rhyme,
though metaphysical and like an epigram.
He who lays his life along the line
will bite the poison pill, and in the throng
the patriot will be anathema.
An afterthought: 'I wish you well.
Goodbye to all pretension. Keep it clean.
Remember Left is Right, and Right is Wrong.
Wipe the gun and polish the machine
and Politics will sing you to your rest.
Keep notes, and nothing more, and make it neat.
The simple honest tone is always best.'
The epigram: 'The shoes will shape the feet.'
Much later, when the season had grown oppressive
with an alien heat, I found myself adrift in the city.
The puzzle glittered in the ruins of the street
beneath a building like a broken tooth.

11

Karl Marx is a comic novelist, almost –
but when we read *Das Kapital* between the jokes we find
there is a theory of religion, then one of philosophy,
a quick adventure and a sordid tale of justice, and soon
a kind of parable emerges like a shadow on a screen:
man is born, grows up and dies. But if this is all he says
we would be cheated, and the authority of the work
is proof of something more than entertainment.
It is like a factory which, on weekdays,
choked and smoking in a frenzy of industry
yet holds prospect of a new revival of the workers,
and which on the weekend sinks into a profound silence
that embodies not only the concept of the modern
forty-hour week, but also the executive's retreat
from that which, though stained and horrible,
provides him with a pretty secretary, a young boy,
a lunch account, and fears of bloody revolution.
(Don't cry at the end of that novel, it's pointless
unless you cry glycerine which is sly and tricky
and all the kids here will love you for it
you witty bastard and envy your 'attack'
or your nerve and pat you on the back and then
leave you to your own devices.)
And think of this: each Russian movie masterpiece
bears his stamp, more than an individual approach,
which is like – uh – like a buried emblem
of the work itself, a tiny mirror for the plot –
or maybe narrative – and in this frame
the image, drift and meaning of the total work
act out their small and wistful life.
Outside this interlocking blazon, a life-style
called 'the film' takes place happily
night after night millions of times
as wasteful and expensive as a Russian dictionary
and more misleading than the tracks it leaves
entering and leaving your life,
and what is that? Snow, politics, the cruel city,
that goodly pedagogic food you ate –

all right, I'm moving, through a dense topography
keeping an eye on how the colourful natives
act out a plausible way of seeing it
for our benefit as we hike away,
leaving behind everything we possibly can.
Getting out is easy, but how you get back in –
say, through a locked window
into a room and a dead love affair
you abandoned the night your future called –
blue moonlight, vinyl floor, lots of mice,
and three creeps in bed – that's different,
that's destructive like a zoo brings tears easily,
so take it easy and forget the lot: Karl Marx,
the parasites, the lovers and the zoo
and run out into the beautiful 'life'
that awaits you. Goodbye.

12

Love is the most awkward game to play. Love
you, and all the wrappings of repair. Move away.
Hate is something closer to the bone, the crooked shank.
Loving You is what the singers say
crying with a mandolin accompaniment
all the way to the bank. Peace has a symbol
like a dove without a cage, and victim to the hawk.
'The olive branch is easily bent,
and rhyme can very sweetly clothe deceit.'
So he, ingesting a drug late at night
in response to biochemical necessity,
constructed a crossword in the shape of an 'Ode
to Genius', in which the legend of a young Poet
screaming in his trendy garret for an ounce of opium
was finally demolished by the smoke
eating into the paint that held his face together...
Love is like a dose of vitamins

13

Maybe you've experienced the feeling of reeling in
a tricky fish? Love is like an angler, or his goals,
obsessively preoccupied with problems of the tide
and plotting out his map against the stars
while fingerlings in countless glittering shoals
play Doctor ('Look at mine!') beneath his keel.
When you're in Love, is that the way you feel?
Love crawls up and knocks you out
and takes you for a ride. While the poet
casts about for the frightful tribes a cold
current is working against him and a vast
tide of frigid water trawls the river bed, stirring up
muddy images and loose packs of themes with needle teeth,
and far across the Pacific, deep in the clouded waters
a movement coloured with despair is working its way
toward the coastal battlements. A sudden squall slathers
ice across his face and in the shrieking wind it seems
that the dead cargoes of all the oceans in the world
swing up groaning from their silty bed and rise
dripping and glistening with deathly light
into the unbearable metal blue of 'Night on the Waters'
where the sea's face is glazed with platinum
and the poem's promise thunders on the broken coast.

14

Nonetheless I am still too young, or
younger than I was, and it's due to a course
of brain-expanding, or younger than that diary
you can see reflected in my dirty window that explains
everything that's gone wrong with civilisation –
it's a forgettable catalogue of folly and pretension,
it's full of gloom and agonised regret and triviality,
it's like a radio play on television, it's like
electric bath-water spilling out of the beach house,
it's more like Mario Lanza than Frankenstein,
though more like Frankenstein than President Kennedy,
and less like President Nixon than a quick fuck.

15

Only ornithologists nowadays write of
blue feathers on a gelid sea
of placid blue, if colours as they theorise
have love of value relatives and ambiguity
and hues are touched with empathy until
they glow with the real uh comparison
of a blue feather on a lake of blue
feathers gelid in the mood of their own unconcern
and 'hating' each other – imagine! hatred tones! – yet
we are stupid because of our binoculars,
our blue spectra and dioptric Ultra Violet
or some other feminine plumage of the 'gelid sea'
so we take a fizzy pill and jump to sleep and
straightaway we become tired in the exhausted
air of our comparisons, and so depart.

16

Perfection of 'the word' whatever
that is, the *oeuvre* of numinous lunch gastronomics
abandoned in mid-choke and throttling on the floor
'like a small and desperate animal' – what can you
make of us, who are so deprived? That we simply guzzle
sound, experience and meaning and are thus disposed
to throw it up? No? That all we mean
is parallels and trizzy metaphysics,
metaphors of loss, we 'quiet ones' who have lost
nothing worse than life assurance premiums?
We who have swallowed 'the best that Western Literature
has to offer', and shat the lot out on the lawn?
Or do you propose to give us holidays
in which we can brush up our commitment?
Plump the flabby pillow of our means? Load one bullet,
spin the chamber, squeak and tickle the trigger and thus
create a new beginning for the literature
of the cultured market gardener and his gleaming wife?

17

Queer, isn't it, how holidays decline
around the rim of a bowl of ratty soup
just so that you and Caroline can make the jump?
And sorry how the idealistic strivings of the young
dribble to a plebbing tack of politics
and tropic mud. But that's the knock, you'll learn to
love it in the end, you and Caroline and Princess
Froth, you and Lady Artemis Gorilla
Sloppy Makeup Throttlegut and all her tribe.
She dives about with copywriters, pokes her tongue,
and giggles in the pool like a randy teacher.
The hi-fi gear is glowing orange with the blues
and Doctor Threat is rolling up your sleeve
for that final pin-prick into yesterday. So choose:
piggy-back the dealer while he teaches you to grease
up that pole, and hope you reach the Muses at the top
and hope you get a good and literary fuck
and if you're nice, a fifty-dollar note. Or get the shits,
hike out through the desert with your awful luck
and take your chances with the butcher's slippery chop.
Look at the snappy camera. Say cheese.

18

Reaching the excuse for verbal intemperance we find
the best argument persuades us to strain out from poverty
to excess, though the profit of this striving
is not in the final chapter but in the zooming
between two worlds of action, neither being of interest
without the gasping towards the other, which is the circus
where we get whatever valuables we come across
and it is not 'reality' nor 'art' that keeps us hot
but the idea of 'hurtling', down the road between
the promise and the thrilling now. This
argument reaches its senility in poetry
for Yeats is said to have composed his most valuable,
fine, and enduring works in flatulent prose
then waited for the scalpel of his intellect and sense
to prong them with the magic clang of verse and wham
bingo they became lasting works of art that students
still can hardly take for granted like a lemonade.
So we end up with a mass of words far more
enduring than a pub bore and twice as sickly,
and our argument smashes through the window
like a trembling ballet dancer scared of rape
but less afraid of broken glass, as we are more nervous
of the poem that might not wriggle into sight
if we declined the challenge of the technique
of cooking 'prose' first and then stamping out
these frilly 'poems' with all their endearing
and 'necessary ornaments of sense'.

19

So there's a dance, and in its alcoholic daze
the Dervish fights his drunkenness;
there is a song whose chords restrict the throat
as music ought. He enters the Gateau d'Ivresse.
It's his Seven-League Boots, this phrase:
'The gangster and his moll'. They meet,
and pass the parcel, and retreat.
'Love? It's just a passing phase.'
Pleasure fits the pockets of his coat.
Slow guitars collect within his gaze.
Dolls, dull stilted birds, a raw
laugh in a jar, the rusty gun.
When the band breaks up his mawkish whore
collects herself. The cheap dance craze is done.

20 (*after R.D.FitzGerald*)

These are not restrictions, but equipment
for use in experiment or exploration
such as it is well to have in hand
when leaving main roads for open country, though
often thrown away in side tracks that lead into
dead ends. Moreover tradition is not just an impulse
out of the past; it is a progressive movement
overtaking the present and helping carry it
into the future. To step aside from tradition could be
one way of being left soon in some small corner
which the present has already deserted. But poetry itself
always sorts out the poets it requires
and gives the best of them their orders;
so despite the monotony of much that is formless
the very incoherence and craziness
of what you have to say are not restrictions,
but machinery capable of jacking up the present tense
and marching it along like a heavy sandwich
into the slobbering mouth of the future.
To step aside is one way of avoiding the collision;
to leap into some small corner is another, though here
in the smog of underlying discontent you find
the older Captains shuffling through their orders
as a paraplegic fiddles with his fly,
and this is the activity of mind
out of which poetry and coloured drinks erupt.

Undo the past. 'One must be absolutely
modern.' Sure, we can abandon sense
and sensibility, and all the disinterred Romantics
like a wicked boy punching in a stained glass knight,
we can be witty partly because of our vodka slingshots
and that's enough to kick the European jukebox in and
get a laugh. But this 'building' thing, this Bildungs-
roman-à-clef, and forests foaming with the puppy love
of seasons... this is architecture, friend, and masterful;
we gape to find the cathedral of words so large
that everyone can find in it the works of his favourite
period, and yet you can always strip that work
of ill-framed accretions and their polyphonic noise
without pulling the whole thing down. Is it plausible
that 'strength' lies in age and British feats of arms?
Are these bits the 'real' cathedral? They might have been,
the whole might have been designed by one man and
finished in the one compelling style, but
'The whole has rather grown than been made.'
Here the jungle is tugged this way and that by armies
of depraved monkeys, for we have reached quandary's end,
surely, as such things have a kind of existence that is
almost midway between the works of art and those of nature.

22

Very moving and persuasive, and too bad the focus
is entirely wrong. To get close enough to grapple
with the problem that lies beneath the problem
that there are no new problems you'll have to crawl
behind the frames in filthy rooms where monsters
fear to think about breakfast in case their hearty
breakfast has eaten itself, and that's nothing
compared to what you'll find behind the scenery,
for surfaces are like chrome in that they rust quickly
and must be scraped away and plugged with fiberglass
thus no mechanic leaves a plane simply polished
but he must have his nightmares confirmed
in flame and crash disaster for lack of digging
into the art of the internal combustion engine, though
we are more like the damaged pilot in his new psychosis
and shall always worry the flight plan to shreds.

23

We could point to the poem and say 'that map',
the heart's geography, and words enact
the muscley parable of exploration: on your right
Maugham's club foot which tromps the clay of life into
a lovely chorus line of English prose; on your left
the dead Romantics, gone into that same earth
that took their tears and all their unforgivable
syntactical mistakes. The land is cruel
with existentialists, though lyric poets
wander through like crippled birds... but this map
is false and crazy – here the Doppler shifts
convert to analogue then back to pulse-code modulation
information full of news and noise, so the heart's
continent abandons form and drifts out into the night sky
full of parachutes, and we feel the mind's mountains
bumping against our head like knobs,
for the little 'heart' grows 'dark' at night
and lacking infra-red photometry and radar
we rave down along the flare path looking like
an anxious moth, don't we? In the flight plan?
But there you go again, plotted out of your simple wit
and this is the second-level problem: observers
without the keys to fit their own responses
so that a poem is merely rhyme and meaning, or a gift
of gaudy trash, and nothing else. So we slog on
to navigate the fading resonance of our capacities
and find the luminescent map of armies
burning on the plain.

24

X-ray breakfast waits for the man who rises
quickly: it's 4:27 a.m. and I'm thinking about
time: life is a mouthful of barium and it's 4:28 a.m.
outside the streets shake with snow pneumonia
it's 30 below and I'm thinking that perhaps poetry
used to be the shot that flung the faulted bone
across the lens, huh? or maybe that penumbra
waiting for the Treatment at 4:29 a.m.
and so forth. It's hard to find a purpose
for that grey machine they wheel in in a sheet.
The time runs out, for 'oranges', asking
who needs the teacher? who needs the magazine? now that
we have the movies and can sit drooling... cobalt milkshake
waits for the thinker who would think his thoughts
deserve the ink they wish to buy. Go on, go out,
be a good guy and buy some 'oranges', get a 'drink'.
I guess I wait around for the Impossible Profile.
Batman! Batman! (the 'Impossible Profile of Desire!')

25

Yet, as the Legendary Profile conforms to a harmony
then falls away from melody to a broken music
you will find a deep attachment to this taste of absence,
against your will you'll be disturbed by the
persistence of the Profile of Desire as it takes on
an enigmatic pertness you could hardly have guessed at
and it will do you no worship to strive against it
for the Profile is more like the tide in its pacifism
and in its bountiful excess as the paradoxical music
develops a lust for the beauty of the ocean and brings
your reachings into disarray for love of its silhouette,
for the Legendary Profile has haunted generations
and brought cities to ruin by its ideology and though
its glance is thrilling, though it seems to love you deeply
you will find it loves all the cities it has conquered
for a short space of time and showers them
with an air of melancholy that is never dispelled
as its nature is to be more elusive than sympathetic,
and though you may hold it in your hands briefly
it will depart again for its working is mysterious
and has a logic like that of holiness
in its frenzy; thus your deeds will have no peace
and your slumber no tranquillity until the Legendary Profile
is brought by you again into the terrible wasteland
it once inhabited and shall now always inhabit
in your grief, by its absence, by its beauty, by the fact
that its piercing sorrow is forever unattainable
once you have touched its lips and faded off to sleep.

26

Zero is the shape of the volcano's orifice
as seen from above, as it is of the human's as seen
from below, and this witless natural joke is a clue
to the purpose, function and economic value of art.
Something like a nothing is what we find
at the final port of call on this cruise when,
stained and weary, we get a flash like a light bulb
blowing up in our face and right there and then
we know everything about life and the creative process.
First there is an accumulated substratum of fact,
and secondly a kind of thermal pressure built up
over decades of suppressed fantasy. Thirdly,
when the whole thing explodes you have an eruption
and millions of gallons of stuff pour out
into colours of hot orange and vivid green,
material which may be revolting and even deadly
at the time, but which forms a useful ground
for supposition in later ages. And so
while the first burst is primitive and spontaneous
after the style of the Romantic gush of the early
nineteenth century, the later consolidations
take on an air of careful structuring
like a policeman blurting out a list of filthy books
in perfect alphabetical order. And that is all there is –
once the Romantic Emotion has ejaculated we find
a vast bed of cooling lava, bare and empty,
giving meagre nourishment to those who follow,
and baneful and pernicious in its influence. And yet
we are still laughing in the jungle, and this
dream of art is nothing but a loony fantasy.

27

After all, we had left poetry behind before this trip had even begun, and all the while we have been bereft of its silly promises of beauty, as the liner leaves the dock and one sees wavelets, sodden streamers in a thousand colours, and some damp flowers drifting downward through the clouded water to that harbour mud; it is as though the coast of South America were never to see us again, and as much poetry as we were able to hint at left as a blur on the horizon as a temporary sign, the more beautiful for being the more easily erased, and even this has strength as it is inevitable and what we have been promised and it is one promise that shall come through: that the slate of verse shall be washed clean, that the South American rivers will drift always to the sea, that the flowers in the mud live and breathe for a short time only and then return us to our dreams.

Starlight

Just under the water sheet you can see
dim grass photographs, two prints
coloured to the temperature of glass
that glint from one sky refraction to another.
Between the surfaces a reluctant prediction
for an invisible childhood, damaged by the future.
Under the glass and the broken starlight
the water stained with darkness

soaks into the earth. Somewhere below
a portrait is moved slightly
by a wish or a failure, to form
omens that point into the past
and indicate 'That promise, how
a tiny growth drains all your effort.'

after *American Graffiti*

Being brave is not enough, this easy
generosity in the loosening grip, in the
strange light which is given off by bottles
when they are tossed from a bobbing boat
and sink, yet do not sink in that
marsh water we have tasted uneasily
and which illuminates our adolescence so that
hot machines are broken and a promise

is a memory as touching as a bad
but well-intentioned movie, though these
artefacts of childhood drifting into age
will never leave us altogether, for our love
even of ourselves feeds on them and on the
endless sorrow of their pressing toward death.

The Bus

My eyes go pale as I grow old, and these
bones, my wrist, are less eloquent than
country radio. I re-live youth asleep
and leave it behind at dawn. In the mirror
there is only me, grey and mumbling.
Who else was in that darkened bus,
driving six hundred miles to a new school?
Only me? I should remember those boys,

but those are photographs, and anxious men
inhabit them; nervous wives cry themselves
to sleep in the country nightfall.
The trawlers are throbbing out of reach,
lost at sea. The mirror clouds over.
The bus speeds through the wet forest.

The Chicago 'Manual of Style'

The Chicago 'Manual of Style' is really neat
when your composure cracks and ghosts
of silly girls come whispering to bother you –
this happens late at night – just kids
out for a bit of fun with a convertible
and a bottle of vodka like in a movie,
and 'Hell,' you think, 'did I do that? Was I
involved with that mad young bitch

the cops were after down at Sunny Point?
Was that me in Dad's truck with the throttle
stuck open, cracking ninety down the beachfront?
With that... brunette... uh?' Just about then,
on the edge of love and terror, the Chicago
'Manual of Style' appears and takes you home.

Pickup Truck

Giving up women is worse than animal laxatives,
it leaves you with a spiritual pain in the head
and conforms its shape to a manual of instruction,
a list of spare parts dealerships in New Mexico,
a mournful gift, and how to fall in love with men.
We got up early to look at the river, or the many rivers
reflected in the multiple prism of the strange air.
Men moved like spoons across the drippy landscape.

Golly, said Helena, there goes my sanity! Indeed,
in full view of the dealers assembled on the bank
she stripped off and jumped into the truck.
It was wet when we got back. I think
if we tape the last few lines into the manual
we've got something useful at the end of the river.

Barnstorm

The cave exists only to be found, and the dark
waits as it has always waited. Chequered aircraft
swing around the pylons in the storm,
my girl leading. She's a good kid. Her eyes
reflect my best pair of empty grey gloves
as a pewter mirror, like the cold
gleaming on the wing. Moisture condenses
in the cave, awaiting tourists or adventurers.

Impetuous planes! The race is over,
three dead, and deep in rainy Cincinnati
the damp newsprint and the metal meet.
My girl passed through the grey parade
with honour, and her Dad clinks her medals
for luck. The Japs move in on the South Pacific.

Landscape with Automobile

The automobile is not suited to the rough
track across the dunes, and soon quits.
I ate fiercely at breakfast right there,
on the sand. The flanks of the automobile
shimmer with metallic heat and echo
when you bump them with your head.
I leaned against them while the stormy fish
gathered below the cliffs in a family

of light, as it was early for the season
to expand in bruised cloud and mottled rain
against the rock wall. I leaned against the rock
wall on my descent, and my thoughts were obscure
in that they shall not be told. I was not
suited to the dunes nor to the family.

The Training Manual

Was I trained to be a nuisance?
The Training Manual is full of homosexuals;
in it you'll find the key concerns
to the great figures of our age.
When they bomb, they are dreadful,
and terror follows them, I think,
like a dog, a carnivore, of equal temper.
Next year, in August, you will fall in love

with a girl who kisses just like Lesbia
who gave a name to an experience
not foreign to the famous or the great.
You, too, live in an empty mansion; in love
you are a child of light, and of hatred,
and you will learn this to your cost.

Art

He was a living legend. He had built
some great structure mainly consisting of art,
though most of those who went through the experience
were knocked around and were inclined to talk about
'a work of skill' and 'admirable diligence',
and thus quite missed the point. Words, paint,
craft, are easily bought, though hard to sell.
Some said he made a million dollars, though

the figure varied, and by the time he got it
he was too far gone to add it up.
Did he really make a work of art?
Did it 'work'? Is it really 'art'?
Is he still alive, or does his 'spirit'
live on in the elegant reviews? Hard to tell.

Artefact

To solve the problem of art and artefact
will you go down to the river
to paint a 'painting'? Will you 'paint'?
Will you paint the girl by the river?
Will you make a painting of the girl?
The light is Grecian, is adequate, et cetera.
He is sitting by the water. No,
he will not paint the girl by the river.

The girl is an artefact, the problem
of the painting is an artefact, is art,
the making of the painting is a problem.
Will you paint a painting of the artefact?
The scenery is well composed, the light
is Greek, is adequate, et cetera.

The Moated Grange

It's bad luck with a coughing baby
and it's just as rough inside the pleasure resort
so don't bother with the Mandrax any more.
You'll get to sleep, and find a business there
that you'll just have to get used to once again.
These palaces you build, or auditoriums,
someone forgot to put the windows in and
all night long you're troubled by a noise outside

so that every day at daybreak you find yourself
asking the keeper 'Was that me? Was that
me and my trouble again?' And he answers variously
according to your face, 'It was a flock of birds,
sir, of red plumage,' or he guesses 'That, oh,
that was you again sir, pleading to be let in.'

The Lessons

Today broke like a china plate,
rain and cloud, drifting smoke;
tonight fell like a suiciding athlete
or a bad joke.
I went to bed with a startling headache
and was distinctly no better when I woke,
I remained dumb in the company of those
who were happy only when I spoke.

Something new has moved uncomfortably close,
something not previously seen:
a talent for aiming the poisoned dart,
for detecting the touch of the unclean,
for discovering that, in the pure of heart,
there is something unforgivably obscene.

A Hard Art

Waiting and waiting, there's an end to it.
Eating bad food, sleeping on the floor,
there's an end to that too. One day
your enemies reach out of your head quickly
and take you to the cold and dirty places,
and you're too old for that sort of thing.
The bad music keeps you there, and makes you cruel,
and you are the loved one you are least kind to.

Waiting and waiting for the good weather,
there's a hard art in that, and a sour man –
too old for that sort of punishment – does it badly.
But one day you wake up and go back home and if you're
tough and lucky you leave most of it behind. Eating
good food, accepting kindness – there's an art in that.

Ballistics

In a distant field, small animals prepare
for sleep, under the huge rising moon.
For foreign peasants, dusk is none too soon.
The bombers fade into the melting air.
In a far harbour boats make for their mooring,
in another town the citizens are glad
the lights are going out. The morning's bad,
the waiting news is cruel, the job boring.

A painter pours a cheap and bitter drink
and drinks it down. His hand's unsteady;
on the table brush and pen and ink
lie scattered. Half his work's no good,
the rest is sold for rent. He's ready;
the loaded gun discharges as it should.

The Museum

The war is over at last
and I have been charged with writing.
I have been ordered to write an elegy,
the dream commands, by bruised boys unable
to command a comprehension of murder.
I am charged with a duty, the committee decides,
to glorify the implements of war! No guilt!
But I make a list of all that is left.

The old world is gone, the Coca Cola
and the benzedrine, the rifles eulogised
and stacked at attention. An old caretaker
is oiling the barrels with a rag and smiling.
The ranks of blued steel grin in the dark.
As much as I am able, I promise the rifles are rusting.

I Know a Man Who Lives in the Dark

I know a man who lives in the dark.
He writes in black ink on black paper.
Whatever he writes is wonderful.
He thinks about history. At midnight
in the light from an ultra-violet lamp
he begins to write. The book will be read
by school-children, he decides, and politicians,
and he considers the struggling republics

and the joys of a country childhood. He paints
a picture of raw youth forged into a legend,
a terrible landscape informed with a sombre glory;
but the ground is a turmoil of combat whose name
is murder. Musing on the republic's favour
he writes a manual on the implements of death.

The Doll

My daughter's playing with her bloodstained
doll again. And the wireless is breathing unevenly
in Frank Moorhouse's novel, grieving that the old
petrol stations are unattended, that all the decent
Rotarians are missing in action in Korea,
the only war to feature the Sabre,
the modern exemplar of warfare,
and the ruthless MiG. It's goodbye to the glue

that used to hold everything together,
it's goodbye to the trembling Rotarians
and their bereaved children in the light
of stinking kerosene lanterns, it's goodbye
to the countryside of honorable rifles.
Welcome the doll, the terrible doll.

Telescopic Sight

In a crude circle of dust and stubbled grass
children are playing soccer. All else
is olive brown and blue reduced to powder.
Outside the boundary the referee
draws a line, cutting off an easy talent
from originality. A small dog like a movie star
drags a grown man across the field,
and his friends follow, asking what to do

with the stricken afternoon, and why is the man
crying. The circle of burnt grass grows
smaller, and somehow the game is accommodated
in the grip of politics. In a dark brick
building on the other side of the world
a man is carefully inspecting a clip of bullets.

The Spy

The spy bears his bald intent like a manic
rattle through the street. A bitter rain
stains the cobblestones. A clock stops; elsewhere
winter tightens up its creaking grip.
Why does the soldier pace the empty field?
Whose war is this, so grey and easily spent?
Slow cars patrol the autoway, children
stare at you cruelly from behind an iron gate

and a brutish gathering begins, somewhere
on the plains far in the hinterland.
The black clock has been still for a hundred years,
and no peasant bears the luck to win
in this poor lottery. Dull green trucks roll out
and the countryside is well advised to be empty.

Passport

A gift to stir up fevered passions,
in a fit to envision a disastrous future
and to tell it as explicitly as possible,
to see through others as clearly as a mirror
but not to see yourself at all,
this is your basic equipment. As for the rest –
compass, map, a traveller's phrase-book –
use them only if you have need.

You have been provided with a wife and child
and a passport, and a respectable position
with a firm of publishers in the city.
As for the stammering, the occasional
failure of nerve... just do the best you can.
Oh – pencil, paper, one-way ticket. Have fun.

The Painting of the Whole Sky

The theme of the magnificent painting
concerns a boy groaning under the weight
of callous governments, and a troop train
moving off to the front. As the train
moves towards the regrettable border the boy
unveils his grief – a whole sky,
storms, and loads of bleeding cloud –
that is his only story, and he cries.

That is to say the train and the wounded
meet like ships in the night. One soldier
loosens a bandage in the wind as the trains
pass in opposite directions. The canvas
flutters, the dried wound freshens, the boys
wave blindly from the painting of the whole sky.

Absinthe

Absinthe breaks down into a type of wormwood,
look how it takes on the Excise Law and comes off
second-best, and imagines in a hundred minds
dun palaces for its own decline. It is new
and easily obtainable, though it's been around;
it would like to be more openly discussed,
though a certain dryness of approach presents
problems for the willing listener – your body

has a chemical glow in the dark, and that
blonde sheen it much admires. Too much
fear comes into the equation suddenly – it is new,
a fizzed-up whore out for a Sunday promenade
as it is hopeful or blue, but never obvious like
'the milk-green lens through which Symbolism shone.'

The Soto Zen School

Once upon a time I had a dream;
I was in a darkened park, alone
with a demented company director
and he was telling me the endless story
of his life (his life hadn't ended yet,
but soon would) – 'When I was ten
I studied meditation with an ancient master
of the Soto Zen school. I wasn't

ready for it. I was too young and anxious.
My head was filled with nightmares, terror
followed me about, and try as I would
I could never "break through". And now I'm rich
and happy, though a little mad.'
With that parable, he left me to my sleep.

The Rhetoric of Fiction

'The Rhetoric of Fiction' is a marvelous thing
being so close to the title of a movie or a thriller
or a brand-name for a patent medicine – this
'blank' verse could easily degenerate
through a slip of the tongue into a fictive
rhetoric too; and so as you become aware
and snap off the radio quickly the room
plunges into silence and there is only metaphor –

'Seen from my head, the reefer on the reef,
distorted to an image of a hunk of beef...'
and you soon realise that you're not alone, you have
the rhetoric of fiction for your adversary; then
there is only the hiss of a cooling valve, as,
inside the radio, a million people are thinking

The Blues

I'd like to throw an epileptic fit
at the Sydney Opera House and call it Rodent.
That's what separates me from the herd.
The hand forgives the cutting edge
for what the hand guides it to do.
The knife has no pleasure in it.
I'm eating my way through my life –
they said it couldn't be done

but here I am in the Palace of Gastronomes
crazy about the flavour!
Moonlight along the blade of a kitchen knife
belongs to the ritzy forties, it's nostalgic
like playing the comb and one-hundred-dollar bill
and calling it the blues.

1968

As you get purchase the hate vehicle
you take another quick look at your sister
and the whole cataract falls into place
under the idea of economy at sea
along the edges of the truck
your sister is playing around smoking
with a nudist drinking pot just
having a real bad time in Jamaica

you know you'll make naked friends
in the twilight you're not sniffing glue
between the Principle of Uncertainty
and the invention of Germ Warfare
there you will find your dazed sister
purchase motor conformity.

By the Pool

James Michener thinks of writing a guide book
to Bohemian Balmain, Sydney, Australia.
People are sick to death of the South Pacific.
He quickly flies to Balmain and has a look.
There it is, like a movie! Writers, artists!
The harbour, blue as always, the container wharves
just like it says in the novels, and the lesbians...
My God, the Lesbians! Bohemia Gone Mad!

This is too much for James, and he flies out.
TOP WRITER JETS OUT OF SYDNEY, AUSTRALIA!
But is that how it really happened? I like to think
of James in the Honolulu Hilton, older and sadder,
nursing a drink by the pool, nursing a broken heart,
dreaming of a pert little lesbian in Balmain.

At the Laundromat

FAMOUS POET JETS HOME TO USA!
How lucky to live in America, where
supermarkets stock up heavily on writers!
Thinking of the famous poets floating home
to that luxurious and splendid place
inhabited by living legends like an old movie
you blush with a sudden flush of Romanticism
and your false teeth chatter and shake loose!

How it spoils the magic! In America no writers
have false teeth, they are too beautiful!
Imagine meeting Duncan in your laundromat –
in America it happens all the time – you say
Hi, Robert! – and your teeth fall out!
And you can't write a poem about that!

The Beach

It's the morning of a summer's day in the inner west of Sydney, the sun already baking the bowl of sky. Here the pollution is heavier than in the centre of town – the sea breeze nudges the smog westwards through the day and into the evening as the lights come on, the evenings of trysts and hamburger smoke and hot cars, the nitrous oxides cooking in the heat and filtering through the lungs of the working classes in the new suburbs on the baking Cumberland Plain stretching towards the outback. You remember that Sydney and Los Angeles are similar the way a rubber stamp is an echo of its image, a coastal plain with an escarpment ten or twenty miles back from the on-shore breezes so that a bowl is formed with a lid of cold air sitting on top of the warm air

And the smog thick with suspended particles and diesel fumes and deadly gas is dumped on the plain right where the people live but the inhabitants laugh, they're happy to breathe the contaminated air that gives them health as well as sickness. And now we've caught the bus and we're moving east towards the coast, the sea, the Pacific, longing for a cool drink –

The buses are blue and white now, the colours of the sky, but they used to be dull green and cream, matching the beach at the foot of the grassy park at Brontë, and made in England, but with the postmodern age Australians tilted toward the Teutonic and the people now go to work in buses made by Mercedes Benz, a name meant to recall the beautiful daughter of a diesel millionaire going to boarding school in Switzerland and having lots of expensive fun;

And now in a flash I remember my first meeting thirty years ago with Stephen Knight – then just a young man fresh from Oxford – in the broiling sun at Tamarama Beach – he lay on the sand in long sleeves, long pants, hat, socks and sandals stretched out in a patch of shade among the sybarites but in the fully-clothed potential of his one day being a professor, even then rolling over in his complicated mind the prolix chilly downhill teleology of Malory's *Le Morte D'Arthur* towards armour-plated death,

So here we are, way back then, a couple of teachers, six young students, a bottle of Pernod, Ferdinand de Saussure and all, dozing and reeling around on the fabulous littoral, the mythological beach –

Hi, Stephen – well at least at an exemplar, one unit selected from the Venn diagram of the immense conceptual set of all the overlapping permutations and combinations of the poems, songs, articles and stories about where the shore meets the sea, and the actual twenty-seven foam-scalloped beaches that bedeck and embroider that doorstep of the South Pacific, Sydney.

The bowl of sand and water is a kind of memory theatre now: when I was a boy in the country I liked to swim, poke at an octopus with a stick and chase poisonous puffer fish through the rippling shallows, then I would wander up the five-mile beach, no one there, squinting against the light reflected from the white sand, a sack over my shoulder, collecting bleached cuttlefish bones to sell to the store for bird feed. One time, walking along a ridge of grassy sand where the hollows are full of heat and stillness, I trod on a snake with my bare feet and got such a fright I didn't think to snap shut the shotgun and shoot. Now the beach seems a tedious gritty way to get skin cancer – just as when I was a kid in a country town I longed to live in Australia's busiest metropolis, Sydney,

And once I got there and failed a few university courses and worked at the Orange Spot Bar midnight till dawn selling the prostitutes fruit-cake sandwiches and mopping the floor, so I travelled, but found London was no better, Iran at least had crystal fresh air

But nowhere to swim let alone a beach,

And in Afghanistan the bell-boy sold you dope for a dollar a handful, but the police threw you in jail if they found you with an alcoholic drink –

Why are we always restlessly searching for a way to help us avoid thinking about the final payment to this charade, death?

In the end, sad joke, it's the wages of fun.

Let's turn back to the landscape – not the real one, this one, which is just a work of art, like something sketched with a pencil and then painted onto a large sheet of paper with those grainy water-colours, the paper crinkling where it's wet – in one sense every artist is just a version of a kid having fun –

But of course there's more to it, namely meaning and characters – once on the radio I heard the art critic Peter Fuller say in his serious English voice 'of course, some landscapes are more meaningful than others', and I laughed so hard I hurt a muscle in my jaw and had to go to the doctor – everyone knows the meaning gets stirred in at the last minute the same way you add mould inhibitor to a can of bathroom paint! and as for characters, just look around you – not at the painted paper, look at Sydney

Sliding past outside the bus window glittering with shops and traffic and its freight of noise and activity, Vietnamese immigrants, here's an Italian family quarrelling, and a Greek fish shop crowded with revellers in white – there seems to be a wedding celebration going on, and the bride's father is yelling at the groom – more characters than you can poke a stick at, every one of them slowly and inexorably heading towards a common end, that unwilling emigration from the country of the living to join the multi-million population of the land of death –

So our feelings write themselves onto the view, turning geography into landscape, distorting the weather. Imagine a sleepy romantic picnic under the trees brought to an embarrassed end with a flurry of leaves and the first pattering drops then the bruised, boiling clouds occupy the sky and a cold rain darkens and fills the summer air

With chill electricity – so we inscribe our feelings onto the backdrop, if a landscape is really a backdrop, the way a young guy in love might notice when he lifts his drink

That it leaves a ring of moisture on the surface of the table and he absent-mindedly traces out a word with his fingertip – a name –

seven letters that are full of magic for him, but not for anyone else in the darkened bar, they're just tired from their day at the beach.

It seems to take ages to get to the coast from almost anywhere, so perhaps we should forget the bus and take the car instead and just put up with the fact that there's nowhere to park and the acres of boiling hot macadam burn the soles of your feet, and when you finally arrive you trudge along the famous golden sand spiked with rusty needles soaked with hepatitis and HIV and junkie spit wondering what the 'style' of the place really represents – you notice the Esplanade is crowded with Japanese brides getting their wedding cheap – they say in Tokyo it costs a fortune with all the presents for the thousands of guests including every fellow worker and all the superiors from the office and their wives, so it's less expensive to fly to Sydney and have the ceremony at the Nippon International and send everyone back home a video – they stroll past the old milk bar that sells Chiko rolls, milk shakes and fizzy drinks, looking for a sushi bar or maybe an American nightclub and trying to get that casual Australian slope into their walk which has been stiffened by a lifetime of restrained competitive frenzy in Tokyo or Yokohama, they walk right by Martin Smith's bookshop and never think to drop in and chat and maybe ask for a bit of light reading... nothing too demanding, you know what I mean, something gushy and fake like *The Piano*, say, to pass the time – their honeymoon time – or a book of haiku about Australian native animals – ha, Aussie Haiku! Excellent! – about native animals, right, but not the ones that creep up inside your trouser-leg and sting and kill, and not the nightmare creatures, say the shark as big as a refrigerator that scoops a leg off in the blink of an eye – you don't feel it for a few seconds, you just feel a heavy bump that knocks you breathless, and then you feel it, and see the spreading red cloud – surely savage predators wouldn't live anywhere near such a crowded beach

And in any case we can see the surf lifesavers patrolling in their kindergarten-coloured caps and costumes and we see the warning poles topped with flapping pennants that spell out the difference between safety and danger more bluntly than the social rules that say you can go just so far with a girl but no further, cravats are in but safari jackets are definitely out this year, and shorts and thongs are not allowed in the Jungle Bar – and a team of hefty lads are dragging a boat into the water, a large elegant rowing boat with half a dozen oars, then they butt through the first wave, the nose lifting up then thudding down onto the water again, it seems to be fun

But it's really a serious kind of work that gives out a noble and metallic social aura because the young men are all volunteers – so are the bush fire fighters with their tankers of life-saving water – here it's the water that kills – and in both cases it's youth facing down the unimaginable that can strike us anywhere and – we hope – defeating it with their strength and guts – you feel a glow of gratitude towards them and plan to buy them all a drink

At the clubhouse afterwards but a gesture like that could be badly misinterpreted, and you notice – as the nose of the boat heaves up into the air again – that some of their costumes are very skimpy, if that's the right word, disappearing into that cleft between the buttocks as the helmsman leans on his oar half-submerged in a boiling green turmoil, the other oars waving in the spray like the feelers of a giant praying mantis – they wouldn't allow that kind of exhibitionism in Melbourne but hey, this is Sydney,

Right? And anything goes – the boat smashes down onto the back of the wave – you duck as a chopper roars over the crowd from somewhere behind the beach and whistles out to sea, rotors flailing the air

And beating the surface to a creamy froth that leaves a lacy pattern of foam as though a huge doily was racing over the water, flying on a mission to protect the eastern flanks of the city from ever-present death.

It's hard to imagine that dark force reaching up and taking you in daylight under the glaring blue sky, death

Belongs to midnight and silence, to the long quiet end of things, to shadowy corridors and empty rooms, to the hospital ward where my father's life leaked away, the starched sheets where my mother's tiny body lay curled in the gloom like a child's, the polished lino floor of the kitchen where my uncle Martin pitched forward and fell, surprised, and in the silence heard his poor battered heart stumble to a stop – it doesn't belong with us gathered here on the sunny crowded beach

With the cries of children and the tinkle of the ice-cream van a few blocks away and the squawk of seagulls filling the windy air.

But death doesn't answer our queries, it doesn't bother laughing at us. It drifts in with the morning breeze, it mixes with the smell of burnt sausages at the family barbecue, with the hiss of gas escaping from a keg of beer, it blends with the chlorine crystals filtering to the bottom of the municipal swimming pool, it blinks in time to the fairy lights and bounces along with the party balloons and the fun

At Mardi Gras and it washes into the gutters that drain the streets of Sydney

And down the sewers into the Harbour and out to the Pacific, a spreading stain, it takes your friends and your enemies alike, and in the middle of the good times it tugs your sleeve and murmurs to you whether you want to listen or not. One summer evening when I tilted into Martin's Bar on Oxford Street – this must be twenty years ago – and asked for a drink

The topless waitress – her pretty tits tipped with pink lipstick wobbling in time to the disco music pumping from the speakers – she asked 'What kind of drink? We've got hundreds,' and I said 'How about a martini?' and she blinked and said: 'Martini, ahh... I know, that's the one with the olive, right? Sorry, pet, we're out of olives, how about a strawberry, okay?' I said 'Are you kidding? A strawberry? Just give me a drink

Of gin with a dash of dry vermouth, please, no strawberries.' And in the shadows a ghost touched my shoulder and whispered in my ear 'Hey, have you tried this? It's better than drink. Friends of yours have gone to sleep in its arms. How about a shot of death?'

No, no thanks, no death. In Sydney

Let's say there's no more dying, each word we speak holds it at bay for one more minute, and where there's a party there's music and happiness, so no dying on and beyond and behind the beach

And in the sloping layers of rented rooms and apartments and human cliffs that stretch uphill, a tilting layer cake made of brick and tile behind Bondi glimmering in the twilight and pulsing with life, under the shade of the trees in the empty avenues, the cars asleep under the street lamps that swap glare and shadow, shadow and glare, you hear the shuffle of stealthy footsteps, clink of a bottle, happy whispering, but no sadness, just a perplexed and sometimes tiring kind of fun,

Okay? – just fun, don't ask questions – in the warm air.

So quick, drop your book, get a drink, breathe in the air and laugh at death. Under the bright blue canopy it's time for fun; it's a summer's day in Sydney, and everyone's going to the beach.

Notes

59 forme – a body of metal type locked into a chase (a metal frame) ready for printing.

71 It's his Seven-League Boots – the last lines of Robert Desnos' poem *'Recontre': (C'est les bottes de sept lieues / cette phrase: "Je me vois".)* The parentheses are included in the original.

72 R.D.FitzGerald – (1902–1987), Australian poet and critic. The stanza is a parody of an article he published in *Southerly* magazine, urging young poets not to abandon tradition.

73 'One must be absolutely / modern.' A line – a paragraph, in fact – in the last section of Arthur Rimbaud's farewell to literature, the prose poem *Une Saison en Enfer*, 1873: *Il faut être absolument moderne.*

73 This poem quotes some scholars on the topic of Sir Thomas Malory's life, his identity and his epic *Le Morte D'Arthur*, authors recommended to me in 1974 by Stephen Knight (see 'The Beach'.)

86 Mandrax – the Australian brand name of a hypnotic prescription drug popular in the 1970s, methaqualone, known commonly as 'Mandies', and known in the US as Quaaludes.

92 'Seen from my head, the reefer on the reef, / distorted to an image of a hunk of beef . . . ' For some reason I cannot now recall, this is a distorted rewriting of a couplet by Robert Adamson about a fisherman.

95 'The Beach' is a superhypermetrical sestina.

SALT POETS

Robert Adamson
Adam Aitken
Louis Armand
Douglas Barbour
Andrea Brady
Pam Brown
Andrew Burke
Maxine Chernoff
Andrew Duncan
John Forbes
Dennis Haskell
Lyn Hejinian
Paul Hoover
Michael Hulse
S. K. Kelen
John Kinsella
Peter Larkin
Anthony Lawrence
Sophie Levy
Kate Lilley
Leo Mellor
Anna Mendelssohn
Rod Mengham
Drew Milne
Peter Minter
Simon Perril
Hilda Raz
Peter Riley
Gig Ryan
Tracy Ryan
Phil Salom
Susan M. Schultz
Tom Shapcott
Keston Sutherland
John Tranter
Susan Wheeler

Printed in the United States
4194